D1337763

Understanding Literature and Film

Interpreting meaning from written and visual media

The Sixth Form College Solihull	The Learning Centre	Stock No 05783
Return by the last date stamped	Don't forget!	Loan Time STANDARD
Ask to renew by phone 0121 704 2581	Or bring your ID to the reception desk	Or e-mail Ask4Info@solihullsfc. ac.uk

Labels V   media

T ✓

Studymates Academic Books

Many other titles in preparation

Studymates

Helping You to Achieve

Understanding Literature and Film

Interpreting meaning from written and visual media

2nd edition

Dr Derek Soles

To Sophie

ISBN 978-1-84285-140-1

Second edition
Published by Studymates Limited
          P.O.Box 225,
          Abergele,
          Conwy County
          L118 9AY

Contents

Preface to the Second Edition

The aim of the second edition of this Studymate is the same as its first edition: to help students achieve a top grade in their A-level and college literature classes. What has changed is the book's content, which has been expanded to include an introduction to the study of film. Film studies are often included now in school and college literature classes. *Understanding Literature and Film: Interpreting Meaning from Written and Visual Media* offers a brief, straightforward, and student-friendly guide to reading and understanding poetry, fiction, and drama, and to viewing and understanding films.

To succeed in your literature classes, you must know the definitions of the various literary genres and sub-genres. These definitions are presented in the first five chapters. You should also be able to recognise and discuss the elements of literature: plot, character, point of view, setting, theme, metaphor, imagery, symbolism, and tone. These literary elements are covered in Part Two of this Studymate. Finally, you need to know the basics of contemporary literary theory. Deconstruction, Marxist, and feminist literary theories are discussed in Chapter 15.

To illustrate the ideas explored in each chapter, *Understanding Literature and Film* discusses, within an appropriate literary context, 46 poems, 19 stories, 4 plays, and 3 films. I have selected those poems, stories, plays, and films which most often appear on reading and viewing lists in school and college literature classes.

Understanding Literature and Film, then, is both a dictionary of literary terms and a guide to understanding selected poems, stories, plays, and films which are frequently assigned in literature classes. I hope this Studymate will help you understand and appreciate literature and help you make a real success of your coursework and examinations.

Derek Soles

Using this Studymate

This book will be a useful supplement to A-level, IB students and those taking literature courses/Access to HE courses at the following universities:

Aberystwyth University First Year Course
Bangor University First Year Course
Bolton University
Birmingham University (MoMD)
Chester University Studying Literature Module
Cumbria University
De Montfort University BA Honours English and Media studies
Dundee University English and Film Studies
Durham University
Edge Hill University
Edinburgh University First Year Course
Essex University Literature, Film and Theatre Studies
Exeter University First Year Course
Glasgow University First Year Course
Glyndwr University
Greenwich University English Combined Degrees
Hertfordshire University English Literature BA Hons
Huddersfield University English Studies BA(Hons)
Hull University English/Film studies
Keele University First Year Course
Lancaster University First Year Course
Leeds University First Year Course
Leicester University First Year Course
Loughborough University First Year Course
Manchester University
Northumbria University
Nottingham University First Year Course

Oxford University First Year Course
Reading University First Year Course
Sheffield University
Southampton University
Staffordshire University
Strathclyde University
Stirling University
Sunderland University
Sussex University
Teesside University English Studies
UEA, First year Course
UHI First year Course
UWE Bristol
Ulster University
York University

1

Introduction:
What is Literature?

Literature is a form of oral and/or written expression which exploits the artistic dimension of language to entertain and enlighten readers. Here are two versions of the same text. One is literature; the other is not.

Kubla Khan

In Xanadu did Kubla Khan A stately pleasure-dome decree: Where Alph, the sacred river, ran Through caverns measureless to man Down to a sunless sea. So twice five miles of fertile ground With walls and towers were girdled round: And here were gardens bright with sinuous rills, Where blossomed many an incense-bearing tree; And here were forests ancient as the hills, Enfolding sunny spots of greenery.	The Emperor, Kubla Khan, built a magnificent palace in Xanadu. The Alph River flowed near the palace through dark and mysterious caves and out to sea. Ten miles of fabulous fragrant gardens encircled the palace. It was an enchanted palace where Kubla Khan heard voices and saw visions.
But oh! that deep romantic chasm which slanted Down the green hill athwart a cedarn cover!	Once I was inspired by a muse to write poetry as beautiful as the gardens of Xanadu.

A savage place! as holy and enchanted
As e'er beneath a waning moon was haunted
By woman wailing for her demon-lover!
And from this chasm, with ceaseless turmoil seething
As if this earth in fast thick pants were breathing,
A mighty fountain momently was forced:
Amid whose swift half-intermitted burst
Huge fragments vaulted like rebounding hail
Or chaffy grain beneath the thresher's flail:
And mid these dancing rocks at once and ever
It flung up momently the sacred river.
Five miles meandering with a mazy motion
Through wood and dale the sacred river ran,
Then reached the caverns measureless to man,
And sank in tumult to a lifeless ocean:
And 'mid this tumult Kubla heard from far
Ancestral voices prophesying war!

If I could get that inspiration back, I would write beautiful poetry again.

I would become a powerful force, capable of changing the world.

People would be in awe of me.

The shadow of the dome of
  pleasure
 Floated midway on the waves;
 Where was heard the mingled
measure
 From the fountain and the
caves.
It was a miracle of rare device,
A sunny pleasure-dome with
caves of ice!

 A damsel with a dulcimer
 In a vision once I saw:
 It was an Abyssinian maid,
 And on her dulcimer she
 played,
 Singing of Mount Abora.
 Could I revive within me
 Her symphony and song,
 To such a deep delight
 'twould win me,
That with music loud and long,
I would build that dome in air,
That sunny dome! those caves
of ice!
And all who heard should see
them there,
And all should cry, Beware!
Beware!
His flashing eyes, his floating
hair!
Weave a circle round him thrice,
And close your eyes with holy
dread,
For he on honey-dew hath fed,
And drunk the milk of Paradise.
 – Samuel Taylor Coleridge

Obviously, the text on the left, the poem, is literature. It is true that both texts are a form of written expression and both enlighten readers. But what about the third component of our definition of literature, 'exploits the artistic dimension of language'? The prose summary is plain and simple; the poem is creative and artistic. The prose version is a house plant compared to the colourful garden of the poem. Coleridge uses vivid imagery, rich vocabulary, rhythm, rhyme and metaphor to augment and intensify the message he is presenting. The prose summary is not striking or memorable; the poem is.

It is the use of language, then, that distinguishes literature from other forms of written expression. The language of a poem is different from the language of a business letter, a textbook or a newspaper. Similarly, the language in a story or a play tends to be more creative and artistic than the letters or the newspaper articles that we read. Storytellers rely on tone, vivid diction and imagery to establish their settings and describe their characters. A play is primarily spoken language or dialogue, but the spoken language in a play tends to be more elevated, more carefully crafted, than ordinary conversation. Some plays, Shakespeare's for example, are even written almost entirely in verse.

To a poet, a playwright and a storyteller, language is more than a medium of communication. It is also an art form. A writer uses language in much the same way as an artist uses shape and colour, to share with the reader/observer the artist's vision of a dazzling landscape, a colourful character, a transforming experience or an intense emotion.

2

Fiction

One-minute overview – Fiction is prose text in the form of a story that is primarily a product of human imagination. In this chapter the fiction genre and sub-genres are defined and illustrated through a discussion of representative literary works. In this chapter, we will explore:

▶ the short story
▶ the novella
▶ the novel.

The short story

A short story is a prose fiction narrative. Prose is the 'everyday' written text of daily newspapers, textbooks and letters. Fiction, though it might be based in reality, is primarily a creation of the imagination, as opposed to a factual reporting of true experience. A narrative is a description of a significant experience in a person's life.

In a short story, the experience usually occurs in a single setting, and concerns a single main character, the story's **protagonist**. Other characters will challenge or support the protagonist as he or she experiences the events which comprise the story. The character who blocks or vexes the main character is known as the **antagonist**. The protagonist usually learns from the experience, though occasionally he or she misses the opportunity to do so. A short story might consist of only a few paragraphs or of many pages, but won't be so long that an average reader could not read it in less than two hours.

Example

Frank O'Connor, 'Guests of the Nation'

O'Connor's 'Guests of the Nation' is a typical short story, often studied in school and college literature classes. The guests, referred to in the title, are two English soldiers, Hawkins and Belcher. They are really prisoners of war, the 1916 war between Great Britain and Ireland. But because they bond with their captors and show no interest in escape, they become more like guests than enemies. They play cards with their captors, converse as equals, and help out with the chores around the house, in Ireland, where the story is set.

Word comes of the execution of Irish prisoners held by the British. In retaliation, Hawkins' and Belcher's guards are ordered to execute their prisoners. No one can believe the absurd situation in which they find themselves. Belcher even offers to change sides. But this is war, and in war the absurd becomes commonplace. The guests of the nation are executed.

The narrator of the story is a young Irish soldier named Napoleon, and his experience guarding two men whom he gets to know and whom he then must execute transforms him. While he does not put his thoughts into so many words, he comes to understand the irrationality of settling disputes by executing innocent men, and, in a broader context, the irrationality of war, especially between two peoples who have so much in common. He realises, as the story comes to an end, that he has changed, that from now on he will see the world and his place in it in a different light.

Epiphany

This change in the main character's values or ideals, often occurring at the end, is a typical element of a short story. This change, this sudden insight or awareness revealed to the main character, is sometimes referred to in literary criticism as an **epiphany.**

The novel

A novel has the same characteristics as a short story but is, of course, longer. An average reader would need at least four hours to read a novel. There is a genre, known as the **novella,** which falls, in length, somewhere between the novel and the short story.

To describe the characteristics of a typical novel, we basically turn the singular nouns of the short story into plural nouns. A novel is a prose fiction narrative, but, unlike the short story, it usually recounts:

- significant experiences
- in the lives of interesting characters
- in a variety of settings.

A novelist has the luxury of a more leisurely unfolding of plot and development of character and novels tend to be less intense than short stories.

Example
Jane Austen, 'Pride and Prejudice'
In *Pride and Prejudice*, Jane Austen tells the story of not one but three romances. These develop over a period of at least a year in several different locales. Her main focus is the development of the relationship between Elizabeth Bennet and Fitzwilliam Darcy. Elizabeth is initially not attracted to Darcy whom she regards as a pompous snob. Darcy is attracted to Elizabeth, however, even though he feels she is beneath him socially. He proposes to her and is stunned to be rejected.

Thereafter, Darcy realises he has behaved badly and he begins to reconsider and change his ways. Elizabeth, too, comes to realise she had prejudged Darcy, that he is more reserved rather than arrogant, and accepts him when he next proposes. He is the 'pride' of the title, and she is the 'prejudice'. After the usual series of misunderstandings and miscommunications, they realise they are perfect for each other, that they complete each other: he needs her to soften his stiff demeanour and improve his social graces; she needs him to learn the restraint and tolerance expected of a woman of her social status.

Counterpoised to the Elizabeth/Darcy relationship are two very different ones. Elizabeth's sister, Jane, loves Darcy's friend

Bingley, and he loves her. But Darcy convinces his friend that Jane is beneath him socially and advises Bingley against pursing the relationship. After Elizabeth convinces Darcy of the error of his ways, he admits to Bingley he was wrong and encourages him to propose to Jane.

Another sister, Lydia, causes scandal by eloping with the dashing young army officer, Wickham. Wickham was one of the most popular of the officers in town, a favourite, even, of Elizabeth's. But his social graces and good looks hide a disreputable character which is eventually revealed. He had no intention of marrying Lydia, but is forced to by Darcy who has known him all his life and who feels some responsibility because he failed to alert the Bennet family to the true nature of Wickham's character.

Typical of a great novel, *Pride and Prejudice* is full of wonderful minor characters who support or harass or put roadblocks in the way of the main characters. Mrs Bennet is the perfect scheming mother, doing whatever it takes, willing to make a fool of herself, to help her five daughters find suitable husbands. The Bennet girls' cousin, Reverend Collins, is a wonderful comic character, an unctuous social climber who flatters, with complete insincerity, anyone he thinks might benefit him. The major recipient of his annoying flattery is the haughty Lady Catherine de Bourgh, Darcy's aunt, who tries to block the marriage between her nephew and Elizabeth, but who, unwittingly, brings them together. So, too, does Bingley's sister who wants Darcy for herself and who therefore never misses an opportunity to criticise Elizabeth behind her back, an activity which only forces Darcy to defend Elizabeth and make him more aware of his love for her.

Pride and Prejudice is typical of the 'happily-ever-after' novel. At the end, those who deserve good fortune and happiness have it, and those who do not, do not.

Tutorial

Progress questions

1. Define, in your own words, the term 'fiction'.

2. What is the difference between a novel and a short story?

3. What is the difference between a protagonist and an antagonist?

Seminar discussion
1. Talk about a fictional character who seems real to you.

2. Talk about a novel you have read that has been made into a
   film. What are the differences?

Practical assignment
Write a personal story that ends with an epiphany you have
experienced.

Study and revision tips
Compile an alphabetical list of the terms important to the study of
fiction. Define each term. You might write each definition out on a
file card to make it easier to sort them alphabetically.

3

Poetry and Verse

One-minute overview – The first task of a student of literature is to learn definitions and characteristics of the major literary categories or genres. Poetry is usually written, occasionally oral, text which accents the metaphorical, imagistic, rhythmic and other aural properties of language. Unlike prose, it is usually shaped into discrete lines of equal or unequal length. In this chapter we will explore the poetry and verse genre, and its sub-genres. Each literary genre and sub-genre is defined and illustrated through a discussion of a representative literary work:

- ▶ regular verse
- ▶ blank verse
- ▶ free verse
- ▶ sonnet
- ▶ ballad
- ▶ villanelle
- ▶ ode
- ▶ epic
- ▶ elegy
- ▶ dramatic monologue.

Regular verse

A regular-verse poem is a literary work written in lines which have the same rhythm pattern and a regular rhyme scheme. If a regular-verse poem is divided into stanzas or verse paragraphs, each stanza will have the same number of lines.

(a) A two-line stanza is called a **couplet**. If the last words in each line rhyme, it is called a **rhyming couplet**.

(b) A three-line stanza is called a **tercet**.

(c) A four-line stanza is called a **quatrain**.

(d) A six-line stanza is called a **sestet**.

(e) An eight-line stanza is called an **octave**.

Rhyme schemes

Each stanza in a regular-verse poem will have the same pattern of rhyme. The rhyming pattern of a regular-verse poem is called the **rhyme scheme.**

Regular-verse poems have a recurring rhyme scheme. The last word in alternate lines might rhyme, the last word in each pair of lines might rhyme, or there may be some other recurring pattern. A rhyme scheme is described by assigning the same small letter to each end-of-line word that rhymes with another end-of-line word. For example, a rhyme scheme described as aabb means that the last word in each pair of lines rhyme; a rhyme scheme of abab means the last word in alternate lines rhyme. Any pattern is acceptable as long as it recurs. In 'Ode to a Nightingale', for example, John Keats used the rhyme scheme ababcdecde for each of his ten-line stanzas.

There are various degrees of rhyme:

1. **Full** rhyme refers to words which rhyme completely: good wood.

2. **Eye** or **sight** rhymes are words which look as if they should rhyme but do not: good mood.

3. **Half** rhyme (sometimes called partial, imperfect, off or slant rhyme) refers to words which sound somewhat alike: home alone.

Rhythm patterns

There are four regular-verse rhythm patterns: **iambic, trochaic, anapaestic** and **dactylic**. A regular-verse rhythm pattern might be interrupted by a pattern used only on occasion, notably the **spondee.**

The iambic rhythm pattern

The iambic rhythm pattern consists of one unstressed sound or beat followed by one stressed sound or beat. The unstressed sound is represented by a 'smile line': ◡. The stressed sound is represented by an angled line: /. Each line of a regular-verse iambic poem will have the same number of beats. A line with two beats – I saw a bird – is called **iambic dimeter**; a line with three beats – I saw a bird up in – is called **iambic trimeter;** a line with four beats – I saw a bird up in the sky – is called **iambic tetrameter**; a line with five beats – Today I saw a bird up in the sky – is called **iambic pentameter**. Iambic metre is the most common poetic metre, suggesting that lilting quality we tend to associate with poetry.

Example

William Wordsworth, 'A Slumber Did My Spirit Seal'
Here is an example of a classic regular-verse iambic poem, 'A Slumber Did My Spirit Seal' by Wordsworth:

> A slumber did my spirit seal;
>   I had no human fears;
> She seem'd a thing that could not feel
>   The touch of earthly years.
>
> No motion has she now, no force;
>   She neither hears nor sees;
> Roll'd round in earth's diurnal course
>   With rocks, and stones, and trees!
>   (1800)

This poem, one of several Wordsworth wrote about a young woman named Lucy who apparently died prematurely, is written in alternating lines of iambic tetrameter (the odd-numbered lines) and iambic trimeter (the even-numbered lines). Its rhyme scheme is abab, cdcd.

Trochaic metre

Trochaic metre is the opposite of iambic. The rhythm of the lines of a trochaic poem consists not of a series of soft-stress-hard-stress sounds but a series of hard-stress-soft-stress sounds. While iambic has a lilting quality, trochaic is harder, more energetic. Trochaic metre pounds upon the page.

Example

William Blake, 'The Tyger'
William Blake chose the trochaic metre for his poem, 'The Tyger', because he wanted to communicate the sense of energy and force which a tiger exudes. To Blake, a tiger is fierce, threatening, deadly, but still beautiful, a symbol of the forceful aspect of God's nature, in contrast to the gentleness of the lamb. Notice, in the first two stanzas of this six-stanza poem, how the pounding trochaic metre reinforces the tiger's fiery energy:

> Tyger Tyger, burning bright,
> In the forests of the night;
> What immortal hand or eye
> Could frame thy fearful symmetry?
>
> In what distant deeps or skies
> Burnt the fire of thine eyes?
> On what wings dare he aspire?
> What the hand, dare seize the fire?

'The Tyger' is written in trochaic tetrameter with a rhyme scheme like this: aabb ccdd eeff.

The anapaestic metre

The anapaestic metre consists of a series of two unstressed sounds followed by a single stressed sound: ˘ ˘ / . It gives the impression of quick movement.

Example

Lord Byron, 'The Destruction of Sennacherib'
Because the anapaestic metre suggests quick movement, Byron chose the anapaestic for his poem, 'The Destruction of Senna-cherib', in which he describes the attack on Jerusalem by a huge

army of Assyrian soldiers under the command of King Senna-
cherib. Notice how the anapaestic tetrameter heightens the sense
of the violent movement of an attacking army:

> The Assyrian came down like the wolf on the fold,
> And his cohorts were gleaming in purple and gold;
> And the sheen of their spears was like stars on the sea,
> When the blue wave rolls nightly on deep Galilee.
>
> Like the leaves of the forest when Summer is green,
> That host with their banners at sunset were seen:
> Like the leaves of the forest when Autumn hath blown,
> That host on the morrow lay withered and strown.
>   (1815)

The balance of Byron's six-stanza poem describes the defeat of
Sennacherib's army by divine intervention. An angel of God
confronts the Assyrians and destroys them all in order to protect
the holy city of Jersualem.

The dactylic metre

The dactylic metre is the opposite of the anapaestic. It consists of a
series of a single hard-stressed sound followed by two soft-stressed
sounds: /ᵁᵁ The dactylic metre is something of a novelty in English
poetry. It is overtly rhythmic and is frequently used in children's
verse:

> Home again, home again, jiggity jig.

Example

Ralph Hodgson, 'Eve'

Hodgson's poem 'Eve' is a rare example of a sedate use of dactylic
metre. The poem describes the temptation of Eve by Satan in the
form of a serpent. The serpent follows Eve around the Garden,
then speaks to her. Eve pauses before she acts:

> Picture that orchard sprite,
> Eve, with her body white,
> Supple and smooth to her
> Slim finger tips,

Wondering, listening,
Listening, wondering,
Eve with a berry
Half-way to her lips.
　　　(lines 25–32)

The ingenuous Eve falls, of course, and is expelled from the
Garden. In this poem, the dactylic metre is very effective in
creating a pastoral but faintly ominous atmosphere which
complements the poem's action.

Varied rhythm and metre
Many regular-verse poems contain lines or phrases which vary the
poem's rhythm pattern.

Example
Gerard Manley Hopkins, 'God's Grandeur'
Hopkins' poem 'God's Grandeur' begins with two iambic feet:

The world is charged

then switches to anapaestic:

with the grandeur of God.

Note how the sudden switch to anapaestic intensifies the
'charging' effect which the poem describes. The next line
continues the anapaestic metre until the last two words, both of
which are hard-stressed:

It will flame out, like shining from shook foil;

The double-hard-stressed phrase 'shook foil' is called a **spondee**.
Poets will use a spondaic rhythm pattern on occasion, usually for
emphasis.
　　Notice, as well, the repetition of the 'sh' sound in the above line.
Repetition of a consonant sound is called **alliteration**. Poets will
use alliteration to create a particular effect. In the line above, the
alliteration suggests the very sound shook foil might make.

'God's Grandeur' continues with a somewhat mixed rhythm and metre. Hopkins' point is that the beauty of nature is a manifestation of God's presence on earth, and that natural beauty will survive despite the way humans exploit nature for their own economic gain.

Example
Wilfred Owen, 'Anthem for Doomed Youth'
Wilfred Owen's 'Anthem for Doomed Youth' begins with two iambic pentameter lines which describe the slaughter of young First World War soldiers whose deaths are commemorated not by the ringing of funeral bells but by the 'monstrous anger of the guns'. The next two lines read:

> Only the stuttering rifles' rapid rattle
> Can patter out their hasty orisons.
>   (lines 2–3)

Notice how the iambic pentameter rhythm is interrupted with the alliterative *r*s of 'rifles' rapid rattle' which actually imitate the sound of gunfire. This is enhanced by the repetition of the 'a' sound in 'rapid rattle' and 'patter.' This repetition of vowel sounds is known as **assonance.**

Blank verse

Blank verse is easily defined: it is unrhymed iambic pentameter poetry. Each line of a blank-verse poem has five soft-stress, hard-stress beats, but the last words of the lines rhyme only coincidentally. Blank verse conveys a formal, authoritative tone. It is quite similar to prose yet it has the aura of poetry. It is familiar, yet elevated language. Shakespeare chose blank verse as the language of his plays; John Milton chose it for his great epic *Paradise Lost*. Blank verse has an exalted history in English literature.

Example
Alfred, Lord Tennyson, 'Ulysses'
Tennyson chose blank verse for his poem, 'Ulysses' because the poem is in the form of a speech Ulysses gives to his crew, and blank

verse is the poetic form which approximates ordinary human speech, while, at the same time, conveying an elevated and formal tone.

Ulysses was the King of Ithaca, a hero of the Trojan War, and the subject of one of Homer's great epic poems, *The Odyssey*. After many years of adventure, Ulysses returns home to his wife, Penelope, and his son Telemachus. Homer ends the story at this point, but Tennyson picks it up and continues. He depicts Ulysses as a man incapable of settling down with his family, eager to set out again on an adventure, despite his advancing years. He addresses his crew, urging them to come with him and 'drink life to the lees' (lines 6–7). By presenting Ulysses' speech in blank verse, Tennyson conveys the sense that a great man is speaking. Ulysses explains his inability to settle down, his desire to continue his journey despite the dangers. He knows he and his crew still have the strength and the will to explore the world some more:

> Tho' much is taken, much abides; and tho'
> We are not now that strength which in old days
> Moved earth and heaven; that which we are, we are;
> One equal temper of heroic hearts,
> Made weak by time and fate, but strong in will
> To strive, to seek, to find, and not to yield.
> (lines 65–70)

Free verse

Free verse is poetry without a set rhyme scheme or rhythm pattern. There might be rhyme in a free-verse poem and there will be rhythm. But there is no repetitive rhythm as there is in regular verse and blank verse and no repetitive rhyme scheme as there is in regular verse.

Example
Mathew Arnold, 'Dover Beach'
Arnold's 'Dover Beach' is a much-studied free-verse poem. It was written in the middle of the nineteenth century, at a time of social unrest. Reform-minded British people were beginning to criticise

the brutal working conditions that even children had to endure in
the mines and factories. Scientists like the naturalist Charles
Darwin were casting doubt upon biblical explanations of the
origin of life.

In 'Dover Beach', Arnold hears the ocean waves beneath the
white cliffs of Dover and compares the ebb and flow of the ocean
tides to the ebb and flow of religious faith. The tide of faith is
ebbing, he claims, in such a confused and uncertain world:

> The Sea of Faith
> Was once, too, at the full, and round earth's shore
> Lay like the folds of a bright girdle furl'd.
> But now I only hear
> Its melancholy, long, withdrawing roar,
> Retreating, to the breath
> Of the night-wind, down the vast edges drear
> And naked shingles of the world.
>   (lines 21–28)

The irregular line lengths and irregular rhyme indicate the free-
verse structure. Notice how the free-verse form helps to establish
the melancholy, pensive tone of the poem and how the irregular
rhythm helps convey the sound of the 'long, withdrawing roar' of
the retreating tide.

As the poem comes to an end, the poet pledges his love for the
woman he is with and begs for truth between them as an antidote
to the sorrow, violence, pain and confusion which currently
pervades the world.

The sonnet

A sonnet is a fourteen-line regular-verse poem, usually written in
iambic pentameter. As a regular-verse poem, it has, of course, a
regular rhyme scheme. There are two main types of sonnet,
distinguished from each other by their rhyme scheme:

1. the Shakespearean sonnet
2. the Petrarchan sonnet.

The Shakespearean sonnet

The Shakespearean sonnet has an ababcdcdefefgg rhyme scheme. Study carefully the form of the following sonnet by William Shakespeare:

> When in disgrace with Fortune and men's eyes,
> I all alone beweep my outcast state,
> And trouble deaf heaven with my bootless cries,
> And look upon myself, and curse my fate,
> Wishing me like to one more rich in hope,
> Featur'd like him, like him with friends possess'd,
> Desiring this man's art, and that man's scope,
> With what I most enjoy contented least;
> Yet in these thoughts myself almost despising,
> Haply I think on thee, and then my state,
> Like to the lark at break of day arising
> From sullen earth, sings hymns at heaven's gate;
>> For thy sweet love rememb'red such wealth brings
>> That then I scorn to change my state with kings.

Notice how the rhyme scheme defines sections of the sonnet, dividing the fourteen lines into four quatrains and a rhyming couplet. The first four lines (abab) describe the poet's despair. The next four (cdcd) tell what the poet envies in others but doesn't have himself. The next four (efef) indicate how the poet relieves his despair by remembering his friend's love. The last two lines form a rhyming couplet; that is, the last words in both lines rhyme: 'brings' 'kings'. Typical of sonnets by Shakespeare, the last lines summarise the sonnet and best express its theme: I realise how lucky I am when I remember I have your love.

The Petrarchan sonnet

The other main type of sonnet, the Petrarchan sonnet, has an abbaabbacdecde rhyme scheme. The rhyme scheme divides the fourteen lines into one octave and one sestet. Here is an example, John Milton's famous sonnet, 'On His Blindness':

When I consider how my light is spent
Ere half my days, in this dark world and wide,
And that one talent which is death to hide
Lodged with me useless, though my soul more bent
To serve therewith my Maker, and present
My true account, lest He returning chide, –
Doth God exact day-labor, light denied?
I fondly ask: – but Patience, to prevent
That murmur, soon replies; God doth not need
Either man's work, or His own gifts: who best
Bear His mild yoke, they serve Him best: His state
Is kingly; thousands at his bidding speed
And post o'er land and ocean without rest: –
They also serve who only stand and wait.
      (1673)

Milton went blind in 1651, at the age of 43. In this sonnet, he wants to complain about the injustice and sense of irony he feels. God gave him the talent to write poetry yet has denied him the light he needs to express that talent. Before he can utter his complaint, however, he senses the voice of God telling him to be patient. God will let the poet know what He expects from those who serve Him. In the meantime, 'They also serve who only stand and wait.'

Because of its brevity, the sonnet is well suited to express specific, pointed themes. 'On His Blindness' is a good example of the sonnet as an effective medium for the expression of a succinct yet eloquent sentiment.

The combined Shakespearean and Petrarchan sonnet

Many poets have written sonnets which combine the Shakespearean and Petrarchan forms or which display a unique rhyme scheme while, of course, staying within the fourteen-line iambic pentameter form which distinguishes the sonnet from other poetic forms.

Example

William Butler Yeats, 'Leda and the Swan'

In 'Leda and the Swan', for example, Yeats builds a sonnet out of two Shakespearean quatrains followed by a Petrarchan sestet. The sonnet describes the rape of the Spartan Queen Leda by the Greek god Zeus who assumed the form of a swan and violated the beautiful young Queen. Yeats describes the rape in the sonnet's first eight lines.

In the sestet, he considers the profound consequences of the rape. As a result of the union between Leda and Zeus, Leda gave birth to Helen of Troy. Helen eventually married Menelaus but was seduced by the Trojan, Paris, who took her back home to Troy. Menelaus and his brother Agamemnon, the King of Mycenae, attacked Troy to get Helen back and so began the ten-year Trojan War. Agamemnon was married to Clytemnestra, Helen's sister, and when he returned home victorious to Mycenae, Clytemnestra killed him so she would not have to give up her lover.

To Yeats, the rape of Leda by Zeus was a cataclysmic event, an annunciation, which marked the beginning of Greek civilization. Yeats' sonnet is atypical in its historical sweep. He manages, in the sestet, to summarise the Trojan War, tell of the death of Agamemnon, and offer a topical comment on the abuse of power.

The ballad

A ballad is a narrative poem, usually written in quatrains. These quatrains usually have:

1. an alternating iambic tetrameter, iambic trimeter metre
2. an abcb rhyme scheme.

As narrative poems, ballad writers often make use of dialogue to advance their stories. Ballads also frequently tell of supernatural occurrences. They usually have specific themes or morals which the author usually presents explicitly at the end.

Example

Samuel Taylor Coleridge, 'The Rime of the Ancient Mariner'

The most famous ballad in the English language, 'The Rime of the Ancient Mariner', by Coleridge, exemplifies all the characteristics of the ballad form. It is written in quatrains which alternate (with an occasional variation) between iambic pentameter and iambic trimeter and it uses the abcb rhyme scheme, as the opening two stanzas illustrate:

> It is an ancient Mariner,
> And he stoppeth one of three.
> 'By thy long grey beard and glittering eye,
> Now wherefore stopp'st thou me?
>
> 'The Bridegroom's doors are opened wide,
> And I am next of kin;
> The guests are met, the feast is set:
> May'st hear the merry din.'

As Coleridge's long ballad continues, the ancient mariner gets his way and compels the wedding guest to listen to his story. The mariner tells of an ocean voyage, interrupted by a storm which drives the ship to the South Pole. An albatross appears to guide the ship, but the mariner impulsively kills the bird with his crossbow. His fellow sailors ostracise him and hang the dead albatross around his neck. The crew falls upon hard times. Another ship approaches and the crew is hopeful until they realise with horror that the ship is a skeleton operated by Death and Life-in-Death. With the appearance of these two characters, Coleridge introduces that element of the supernatural common in ballads. The two ghastly characters roll dice to determine the fate of the crew. Death wins the crew who begin to drop dead; Life-in-Death wins the ancient mariner.

The mariner suffers as if he were in hell. Then he turns his attention to God's creatures swimming in the ocean below him. He thinks how beautiful they are, and he subconsciously blesses them. Having thus re-established his respect for nature, the mariner is rewarded:

> A spring of love gushed from my heart,
> And I blessed them unaware:
> Sure my kind saint took pity on me,
> And I blessed them unaware.

That selfsame moment I could pray;
And from my neck so free
The Albatross fell off, and sank
Like lead into the sea.
  (Part 4, lines 284–291)

Rain comes, the dead crew temporarily comes back to life, inhabited by the spirits of angels, and the mariner makes it back to England. As part of his punishment and rehabilitation, he is compelled to tell his story to people like the hapless wedding guest whom the mariner senses will most benefit from his tale of the dire consequences which threaten those who do not respect nature. The ballad's ending is typical of the genre in that it ends with a specific statement of the poem's theme:

'He prayeth best, who loveth best
All things both great and small;
For the dear God who loveth us,
He made and loveth all.'

The Mariner, whose eye is bright,
Whose beard with age is hoar,
Is gone: and now the Wedding-Guest
Turned from the bridegroom's door.

He went like one that hath been stunned,
And is of sense forlorn:
A sadder and a wiser man,
He rose the morrow morn.
  (Part 7, lines 614–625)

The villanelle

A villanelle is a nineteen-line poem divided into five tercets and one quatrain. It has a very specific structure. It has:

1. an iambic pentameter rhythm and metre
2. an aba aba aba aba aba abaa rhyme scheme.

The first line of the first tercet of a villanelle is repeated as the last line of the second and fourth tercets. The last line of the first tercet is repeated as the last line of the third and fifth tercets. These two lines, the first and third of the first tercet form a rhyming couplet at the end of the poem.

Example
Dylan Thomas, 'Do Not Go Gentle'
Thomas's poem 'Do Not Go Gentle Into That Good Night' is without doubt the most frequently anthologised villanelle in the language. In the poem, Thomas urges his dying father, a gentle man, to fight death:

> Do not go gentle into that good night,
> Old age should burn and rave at close of day;
> Rage, rage against the dying of the light.
>   (lines 1–3)

Notice how the iambic rhythm is broken by the powerful spondee 'Rage, rage' in the third line.

Thomas goes on to describe stereotypical men – wise men, good men, wild men and grave men – in stanzas two to five respectively, explaining to his father how they all regretted something about the way they lived their lives and, as a result, resented death and fought against it. In keeping with the villanelle format, the last lines of the second and fourth tercets are identical to the poem's opening line; the last lines of the third and fifth are identical to the last line of the first tercet.

As the poem comes to an end, Thomas urges his father to follow the leads of those wise, good, wild and grave men, and fight against death:

> And you, my father, there on the sad height,
> Curse, bless, me now with your fierce tears, I pray.
> Do not go gentle into that good night.
> Rage, rage against the dying of the light.
>   (lines 16–19)

The ode

An ode is a long formal poem which usually presents a poet's philosophical views about such subjects as nature, art, death and human emotion. Most odes are written in regular verse; some are in free verse.

Example of a regular-verse ode
John Keats, 'Ode to a Nightingale'
Keats' odes are among the most famous regular-verse odes in the English language. 'Ode to a Nightingale' is a typical Keats ode. It is a poem of eighty lines, divided into eight stanzas of ten lines each. The lines have an iambic pentameter rhythm (broken in line 8 by a line of iambic trimeter) and an ababcdecde rhyme scheme.

Odes often concern the relationship between the human and natural worlds. Keats addresses this ode to a nightingale whose song symbolises the permanence of nature, in contrast to the impermanence of human existence. The ode describes the poet's desire to escape from a life which is filled with hardship and join the nightingale in the peaceful, beautiful and eternal world which resonates within its own incomparable song. Keats wanted so much to share in such a world because his own was so tragic. He was terminally ill with tuberculosis, an illness which had already taken his young brother, Tom. Keats alludes to Tom's death in Stanza 3, wherein he describes the sorrow and brevity of life as he knows it:

> Where youth grows pale, and spectre-thin, and dies;
>   Where but to think is to be full of sorrow
>   And leaden-eyed despairs;
> Where Beauty cannot keep her lustrous eyes,
>   Or new Love pine at them beyond to-morrow.
>   (Stanza 3, lines 26–30)

Understandably, he longs for a place without pain and suffering and thinks he can find it within the nightingale's mystical realm. He reaches that place and it turns out to be all he had hoped for. In stanzas five and six, Keats describes the intoxicating scent of the flowers, the ecstatic song of the nightingale, and the sense of immortality he feels there.

But he knows his escape is only temporary. As the nightingale's song fades, the poet is jolted back to reality. 'The fancy cannot cheat so well/ As she is famed to do,' he says in the final stanza. He is left somewhat disoriented by the whole intense experience.

'Ode to a Nightingale', typical of its genre, is a contemplation on life and death, the human and the natural. Also typical of the English ode is its reflective tone, tinged with sorrow and resignation.

Example of a free-verse ode

William Wordsworth, 'Ode: Intimations of Immortality'
While most odes are written in regular verse, a few are in free verse. The most famous free-verse ode in English is Wordsworth's 'Ode: Intimations of Immortality'. It is a 203-line poem divided into eleven stanzas of various length and rhythm. Wordsworth uses rhyme extensively within each stanza but the poem does not have a repetitive rhyme scheme.

Wordsworth begins his poem by reflecting on his past, specifically the joy he experienced as a child communing with nature. Now, as an adult, that spontaneous joy has passed and he yearns to get it back. For several stanzas, four to eight, Wordsworth celebrates the beauty and innocence of childhood, a time of freedom, and innocence bolstered by a naïve belief in immortality.

Inevitably, though, the innocence of childhood gives way to the responsibility of adulthood. Adulthood is burdensome compared to the freedom of childhood, but Wordsworth does not dwell on the negative. Instead, he finds comfort in remembrance of things past:

> Though nothing can bring back the hour
> Of splendour in the grass, of glory in the flower;
> We will grieve not, rather find
> Strength in what remains behind;
> In the primal sympathy
> Which having been must ever be;
> In the soothing thoughts that spring

Out of human suffering;
In the faith that looks through death,
In years that bring the philosophic mind.
(Stanza 10, lines 177–186)

Wordsworth's 'Immortality Ode' has the same quiet, philosophical, reflective tone as 'Ode to a Nightingale'. Like Keats' ode, it
focuses on nature and the lessons we can learn by examining our
relationship with the natural world. Wordsworth's ode is more
upbeat than Keats', however, ending as it does with the sense that
the wonder of childhood has been superseded by a more mature
and realistic view of life.

The epic

An epic is a narrative poem, about the length of a long novel. It
has a traditional structure. An epic typically opens in the middle of
the action – the literary term is *in medias res*. It continues
chronologically through several events, then flashes back to the
beginning of the story, and finally jumps back to the point where
the flashback began and continues the story to its conclusion.

Epic poems always include both mortal and supernatural
characters who regularly interact. The poet begins by invoking a
supernatural power to help him tell his story. Supernatural
characters – gods, goddesses, angels – intervene in the lives of
mortal characters either to help them achieve a goal or to thwart
their plans and aspirations. A god, goddess or angel will typically
warn a mortal character before a cataclysmic event takes place.

Examples
Homer
The plot of an epic poem usually focuses on warfare, its causes and
its consequences. Homer's great epic *The Iliad* describes the siege
of Troy by Greece and her allies. *The Odyssey*, also by Homer,
describes the adventurous voyage home after the Trojan War of
Odysseus, King of Ithaca. Virgil's famous epic *The Aeneid* tells of
Aeneas's escape from the Greeks at the end of the Trojan War and
his harrowing journey to his homeland, Italy.

John Milton, 'Paradise Lost'

In the English language, a great epic poem is John Milton's *Paradise Lost*. *Paradise Lost* opens in Hell where Satan announces to his fellow fallen angels that God is planning to create a whole new world. Satan and his followers agree that they can spoil God's plan and be avenged for their defeat by corrupting man who will inhabit God's new world. Satan sets out on the mission. He persuades Sin and Death to unlock the Gates of Hell so he can proceed. He tricks the archangel Uriel into revealing the location of the Garden of Eden. Disguised as a cormorant, he spies on Adam and Eve from the Tree of Life at the edge of the Garden. He learns about the Tree of Knowledge on which grows the forbidden fruit.

The archangel Gabriel learns of Satan's presence in the Garden and sends three angels to protect Adam and Eve. Satan leaves, but not before putting a dream in Eve's consciousness about the pleasure of tasting the fruit of the forbidden tree. God sends his angel Raphael to warn them about Satan and to remind them that He gave man free will so Adam and Eve might fall from grace. Raphael also tells them the story of man's creation. Chronologically, the epic begins at this point.

Satan returns to the Garden, assumes the form of a serpent and tempts Eve to taste of the forbidden fruit. She does so and convinces Adam to do the same. They have knowledge now of evil, and their personalities and actions change accordingly. God sends his Son to the Garden to pass judgement on Adam and Eve. He forgives them but foretells a bleak future. The archangel Michael arrives to lead them out of the Garden. He offers them hope, as the epic ends, promising that the Son of God will come to earth to redeem man's sins.

Paradise Lost, in keeping with the epic genre, tells the ultimate human story: the battle between good and evil, more specifically the triumph of good over evil. The temptation to sin is irresistible; if Adam and Eve were sinners, so are we all. But because sin is redeemed through (in this epic) the Christian values of love, compassion, temperance and devotion, good will triumph in the end. Ultimately, Adam and Eve's expulsion from the Garden is less tragic than bittersweet, in that they leave with the knowledge that faith in the Redeemer who will come can lead them back to Paradise.

The elegy

An elegy is a poem written to commemorate the death of a person who played a significant role in the poet's life. Famous elegies include:

▶ Percy Bysshe Shelley's 'Adonais' in memory of the death of John Keats

▶ Alfred Lord Tennyson's 'In Memoriam', written to commemorate the death of his friend, Arthur Hallam

▶ 'Lycidas', John Milton's homage to his friend Edward King.

These poets praise the virtues of their friends and often use the occasion of their friends' deaths to comment on the role fate plays in an uncertain world. A **pastoral elegy** (such as 'Adonais' and 'Lycidas') typically contrasts the serenity of the simple life of a shepherd with the cruel world which hastened the death of the poet's friend.

Example

W. H. Auden, 'In Memory of W. B. Yeats'

Auden's 'In Memory of W. B. Yeats' is the best-known elegy written this century. This poem expresses sorrow, tempered by the realisation that Yeats will live on through his work and the many readers who admire it. Typical of the genre, this elegy contrasts Yeats' wisdom with the greed and dispassion of the modern world. The poem was written on the eve of the Second World War:

> In the nightmare of the dark
> All the dogs of Europe bark,
> And the living nations wait,
> Each sequestered in its hate;
> (lines 46–49)

A poet's art, Auden suggests, transcends war's hate, heals the bruised soul, and lets 'the healing fountain start' (line 63).

The dramatic monologue

A dramatic monologue is a poem which is 'dramatic' in the sense that it is a speech presented to an audience (sometimes of only one person) and a 'monologue' in the sense that no other character does any talking. Some dramatic monologues, such as T. S. Eliot's 'The Love Song of J. Alfred Prufrock', are written in free verse; others, like Robert Browning's 'My Last Duchess', are in regular verse; and some, like Tennyson's 'Ulysses', are in blank verse.

Example
Alfred, Lord Tennyson, 'Tithonus'
'Tithonus' is another important blank-verse dramatic monologue by Alfred, Lord Tennyson. Tithonus was a Trojan prince, loved by Aurora, the goddess of the dawn. Aurora prayed to the gods to make Tithonus immortal, and her prayers were answered. Unfortunately, she did not ask that Tithonus be granted the gift of eternal youth. Tithonus grows so old and withered, he can no longer bear his life, and he begins to yearn to die. In this dramatic monologue, Tithonus asks Aurora to 'take back thy gift' (line 27). He is surrounded by matchless beauty, one of the advantages of being the roommate to the goddess of the dawn. Yet he wants to be a man again and 'have the power to die' (line 70). 'Tithonus' is a dramatic monologue that validates the nature of the human life-cycle, the decay of the body and the concomitant release of the spirit.

Tutorial

Progress questions
1. Define, in your own words, the term 'poetry'.

2. What is the difference between a Shakespearean and a Petrarchan sonnet? Between a regular-verse ode, and a free-verse ode?

3. How do rhythm, rhyme and metre each contribute to the meaning of a poem?

Seminar discussion
1. Do you, personally, prefer to read poetry silently or out loud? Why?

2. Poetry is often thought of as the 'least accessible' literary genre. Do you agree or disagree with this assessment?

Practical assignments
1. Read one other literary work which is an example of each of the poetry and verse sub-genres discussed in this chapter.

2. The major, but not all of the poetry and verse genres have been covered in this chapter. Try to find one which has not been discussed and make a few notes on its characteristics.

Study and revision tips
Compile an alphabetical list of the poetry and verse genres and their definitions. You might write each definition out on a file card to make it easier to sort them alphabetically.

4

Drama and Theatre

One-minute overview – The first task of a student of literature is to learn definitions and characteristics of the major literary categories or genres. As we have seen, there are three main literary genres, fiction, poetry and drama. Drama is performance text, a story told through the dialogue of its characters and presented in front of a live audience. Like the others, this major genre subdivides into a number of sub-genres. In this chapter we will define and illustrate them through a discussion of a representative literary work:

▶ tragedy
▶ comedy
▶ the theatre of the absurd.

Tragedy

The tragic hero
As a literary genre, a tragedy is a play which tells the story of a significant event or series of events in the life of a significant person. This person is called the **tragic hero**. The tragic hero is usually a man, though notable exceptions include Shakespeare's Cleopatra and Juliet, and Sophocles' Antigone. The tragic hero is usually a member of the nobility: a king, a prince or an emperor. He is well-respected within his community, a leader, a wise, just and good man.

But the tragic hero is human and, as such, is imperfect. The tragic hero has a character defect, called the **tragic flaw** or **hamartia**. He might be arrogant or too impulsive or indecisive or insecure. This flaw, whatever it is, causes many problems which snowball and ultimately result in catastrophe for the very community the tragic hero should be leading.

In keeping with this movement towards catastrophe, brought on by the tragic hero's hamartia, the plot of a tragedy tends to move from bad to worse because of the tragic hero's errors in judgement, even though the errors are unwitting. The disaster might be a plague, widespread civil unrest, or a general atmosphere of distrust and suspicion. The misplaced actions (or lack of action) of the tragic hero causes or contributes in a major way to the disaster. In a tragedy there is a general sense that the cards are stacked against the tragic hero and the world in which he lives, that he is the victim of a malign fate.

The scapegoat

In the interests of the restoration of the community, the tragic hero must go. A tragedy will typically end with the death or the exile of the tragic hero. Thereafter, life in the community begins to get back on track. The tragic hero, then, is ultimately a scapegoat. A **scapegoat** is a person who is banished or sacrificed in the interests of his community. Typically, the scapegoat atones in some way for his sins and for the sins of his people. The concept of sacrifice, of the 'scapegoat', is central to the definition of tragedy. The word tragedy comes from the Greek word meaning 'goat's song'.

Catharsis

Paradoxically, a tragedy is not, in the end, an occasion for sorrow, but more an occasion for relief. The audience witnesses disaster and despair acted out before them. They are moved to pity for the tragic hero and anger at a world which can seem to be so heartless. At the end of the play, the audience releases this pity and anger. They feel better, then, for having purged body, mind and soul of pent-up emotions.

This purgation of audience emotion is central to the theory of tragedy. It is known as the **catharsis**. Catharsis is not something that happens to the characters in the play; it is the very heavy collective sigh of both grief and relief the audience heaves, as the tragic hero is defeated and as, in the wake of that defeat, order returns to his world.

Example of a tragic drama

William Shakespeare, 'Hamlet'

Shakespeare's *Hamlet* is the most frequently taught and anthologised English tragedy. The plot of the play is typical of the genre in that fate seems to conspire against any chance of harmony and happiness.

Hamlet is the story of the murder of the King of Denmark, and the attempt by the Prince Hamlet to avenge his father's murder. The murder was committed by Hamlet's own uncle, his father's brother, Claudius, who murdered the King to take over the throne and marry the Queen, Hamlet's mother, Gertrude. The murder devastates Hamlet who falls into a depression and ends his relationship with his girlfriend, Ophelia.

Hamlet agonises over his duty to avenge his father's 'foul and most unnatural murder', largely because he learned of the crime from the ghost of his father, and ghosts cannot always be trusted. He establishes Claudius's guilt, however, by tricking Claudius, in a most ingenious way, into revealing his guilt. Still, his attempts at revenge are thwarted. He kills, by accident, his uncle's chief adviser Polonius, Ophelia's father, and he is sent into exile. By now Claudius is certain Hamlet intends to kill him.

Hamlet manages to get back to Denmark, however, to try again. Polonius's son, Laertes, challenges Hamlet to a duel and conspires with Claudius to poison his blade to effect Hamlet's death. In the course of the duel, both Hamlet and Laertes are wounded with the poisoned sword, and Laertes then reveals Claudius's treachery. Before the poison ends his life, Hamlet stabs Claudius and forces down his throat a glass of poisoned wine, meant for Hamlet, in the event that the poisoned sword did not work. Meanwhile, Gertrude has also died, having innocently drunk some of the poisonous wine. As the play ends, the new King of Norway arrives to restore order within the rotten state of Denmark.

Hamlet is the archetypal tragic hero. He is a handsome, intelligent young Prince, an expert swordsman, and loved by the people of his country. His tragic flaw, however, is his lack of emotional balance. Hamlet's engine has two gears: stop and charge. He either acts rashly, without thinking, as when he kills Polonius and attacks Laertes at Ophelia's funeral, or he does not act expeditiously enough. He never gets around to killing Claudius and avenging his father's murder until the end of the play when it is really too late. Up until that point, Hamlet philosophises about death, ponders the consequences of his actions, finds excuses to stonewall, and waxes poetic about all manner of subjects. He does not act quickly and firmly enough. Hamlet admires his friend Horatio because Horatio has that balance between reason and emotion Hamlet knows he needs but cannot attain. This lack of balance, especially his tendency to talk too much and act too slowly, causes his downfall. Man is free to act, say the existentialists, but man must act to be free.

The imagery in *Hamlet* reflects and augments the atmosphere of corruption and hypocrisy which pervades Denmark, governed as it is by a King who murdered his own brother. Images of decay and disease validate Marcellus's claim, early in the play, that 'something is rotten in the state of Denmark.' Images of concealment, of women hiding their true selves behind thick makeup, of 'sugaring over the Devil himself', of outward appearance masking inward treachery highlight the hypocrisy which runs rampant throughout a kingdom where almost everyone is something other than what he or she appears to be.

The end of the play brings relief, catharsis, as a tragic ending must. We grieve at the deaths of Hamlet and Ophelia, accept the death of Claudius, and know that with the arrival of Fortinbras, literally 'strong in arms', Denmark will return to the rule of law and good government.

Comedy

Comedy is, in most ways, the opposite of tragedy.

▶ *Plot* – The plot of a comedy moves not from bad to worse but from bad to good. Typically, in a comedy, young men and women want to come together but are prevented from doing so by a variety of obstacles which range from bad luck to unyielding adults. In the end, though, the luck changes, those who would block the union are thwarted, the young people marry and live happily ever after.

▶ *Characters* – In a tragedy the main characters are generally serious and solemn and one character, the tragic hero, dominates the action. In a comedy, the main characters remain upbeat no matter what fate brings them, sensing that in the end they will triumph.

▶ *Stereotypes* – In a comedy, the characters tend to be stereotypical, which means they are recognisable *types* of people rather than fully developed characters like the tragic hero. Common stereotypical characters include the dumb blonde, the man who thinks he is God's gift to women, the miser, the fickle young lover, the lazy slob, the rich spoiled child, the social snob. Those characters who try to prevent the union of the young people are referred to as **blocking agents**.

▶ *Dramatic spirit* – The spirit of comedy is different from the spirit of tragedy. In a comedy, there is always a sense that everything will turn out well, despite the horrible predicaments the characters find themselves in.

Example
Oscar Wilde, 'The Importance of Being Earnest'
Wilde's *The Importance of Being Earnest* is a much taught, much anthologised comedy. It is the story of two young men and two young women who want to get engaged but can't because circumstances stand in their way. Gwendolen's mother, Lady Bracknell, won't let Gwendolen marry John because John has no real family. In fact, he was discovered in a train station as a baby and raised by a philanthropic country gentleman. Gwendolen loves John, mainly because she thinks his name is actually Ernest, her favourite name.

The other couple in the play are Algernon and Cecily. Algernon wants to marry Cecily but can't because his best friend is her guardian and that friend – who is, of course, John – thinks Cecily is too young and Algernon too experienced, and he refuses to agree to the union. Cecily loves Algernon because she believes he is actually John's reprobate brother, Ernest, which happens to be not only Gwendolen's but her favourite name as well.

In the end, the problems are resolved, and the true identity of John is discovered. He is, of course, Algernon's older brother, and his real name is, of course, Ernest.

The characters in *The Importance of Being Earnest* are typical comic stereotypes. Lady Bracknell is the blocking agent, a hilariously supercilious meddlesome mother. John and Algernon are spoiled young aristocrats who don't have to work for a living. They spend their time dining at the right places, shopping for the right clothes, and flirting with eligible young women. Their counterparts are Gwendolen and Cecily, fickle and superficial, frivolous, rich and spoiled young women.

Typical of a comedy, *The Importance of Being Earnest* makes us laugh with the witty banter and sarcasm which the characters exchange. It has the typical ingredients of the classical comedies: mistaken identity, explained away at the end; an abandoned baby who turns out to be related to another character; young people whose energy and enthusiasm conquer anything that stands in the way of their happiness.

The theatre of the absurd

'Theatre of the absurd' is a phrase used to describe a group of plays written during and after the 1950s. The term 'absurd' is used because the plots and the characters (though not the themes) are unconventional compared with conventional tragedy and comedy. The characters are eccentric, and their speech and their actions often seem unintelligible. The plots are often static; any forward movement that does occur is usually reversed by the time the play ends. The themes are the predictable issue of the plot and characters, bleak in their obsession with the hopelessness of the human condition, yet intriguing and thought-provoking at the same time.

Example
Samuel Beckett, 'Waiting for Godot'
Samuel Beckett's *Waiting for Godot*, which opened in Paris in 1953, is usually considered to be the first theatre-of-the-absurd play, and it remains one of the most widely anthologised and taught.

The play is set on a deserted road where two apparently homeless and derelict men, Vladimir and Estragon, are waiting for a third man, Godot, though they are not sure exactly why they are waiting for him. They talk about sore feet, they try to remember the story about the thieves executed with Christ, and they even consider hanging themselves from the one tree on their desolate road. They smile because 'one daren't even laugh any more'. They reach the conclusion: 'Nothing to be done'. They wait.

Two new characters, Pozzo and Lucky, arrive. Lucky has a rope around his neck and Pozzo is driving him forward using a whip. Vladimir and Estragon are in awe of Pozzo's power over Lucky. Pozzo orders Lucky to perform for them, specifically to 'think'. Lucky's famous 'think speech' is, predictably rambling and meaningless, though, typical of a theatre-of-the-absurd play, some statement about human faith or faithlessness does seem to struggle to emerge from between the lines. Pozzo and Lucky leave. A young boy enters with a message from Godot: he is not coming tonight, 'but surely tomorrow'. Vladimir and Estragon decide to go but do not move.

The opening of Act II, which apparently takes place the next day, is a recapitulation of Act I, except the tree now has a few leaves on it. Vladimir notices the change as the pair sit down to wait again for Godot. They are not sure if it is the same tree, if time has passed, or if they are in the same place. They reminisce about their days picking grapes in a beautiful valley so different from the wasteland they now inhabit. They find a hat, apparently belonging to Lucky, and play with it for a while. They call each other mean names, as a way of passing time. Estragon begs for God's pity. Pozzo and Lucky arrive on the scene again, this time in altered circumstances. Pozzo is blind and Lucky is mute, the rope is much shorter than it was in Act I, and Lucky carries suitcases full of sand. They fall down, and, in trying to help them back up, Vladimir and Estragon fall down as well. Eventually, Pozzo and Lucky struggle up and continue on their journey, and the other two are left alone with their despair once again. A messenger arrives with the news that Godot will not come this evening but will come tomorrow. They consider hanging themselves again but Estragon has forgotten the rope and the cord holding up his pants is too weak. They resolve to hang themselves tomorrow if Godot does not come. They decide to go but, again, do not move.

The main theme of *Waiting for Godot* is the loss of faith in the modern world and the human inability to find something to replace God(ot). Some people, like Vladimir and Estragon, wait for salvation; others, like Pozzo and Lucky, attempt to find faith in the material world instead – an attempt which exploits one of them and eventually grinds both of them, quite literally, down.

The breakdown of communication is another important theme of the play, evident in the characters' difficulty in sustaining a conversation with each other and in Lucky's parody of intellectual discourse. Paradoxically, and typical of a theatre-of-the-absurd play, there is much meaning in the characters' inability to find meaning in their lives, devoid as they are of faith, hope and charity and drawn to the consideration of their own deaths. Theatre of the absurd dramatists place characters in settings and situations which are, on the surface, absurd, but which represent real social issues which need to be addressed.

Tutorial

Progress questions
1. Define, in your own words, the term 'drama'.

2. What are the key differences between a tragedy and a comedy?

3. What is meant by an archetype? A stereotype?

Seminar discussion
1. Is a theatre-of-the-absurd play more like a tragedy or a comedy or is it a combination of both?

2. Do you, personally, prefer to read poetry or fiction or watch a live play? Explain your answer.

Practical assignments
1. When you have the chance, go to see a live play and watch it in the light of what you have learned about the conventions of a tragedy, a comedy, or theatre of the absurd.

2. Read one other literary work which is an example of each of the dramatic sub-genres discussed in this chapter.

3. The major, but not all of the dramatic sub-genres have been covered in this chapter. Try to find one which has not been discussed and make a few notes on its characteristics.

Study and revision tips

Compile an alphabetical list of the dramatic genres and their definitions. You might write each definition out on a file card to make it easier to sort them alphabetically.

5

Film

One-minute overview: In the last chapter, we learned that drama is the least print-based of the literary genres. You likely will read and study the text of a play in your literature classes, but you will soon realise the limitations of studying drama this way. Drama is more a visual than a print medium. When you see a play performed, you get a quite different perspective of its action, setting, and characters than you do if you simply read the text of a play. As an audience member, you experience all of the play at once; you don't read 20 pages one day, another 40 the next, and so on. Moreover, the director's interpretation of the play's theme (see Chapter 10) and the actors' interpretation of the characters; the props and scenery the set designer builds and the clothes the costume designer puts on the actors; the artistry of the sound and lighting technicians – these and other technical features will colour your perception of the experience, your understanding of the play. Poetry and fiction engage our senses profoundly but indirectly and subconsciously; live drama engages our senses more viscerally.

If drama is the least print-based of the literary genres, **film** is the least print-based of the dramatic arts. Certainly, it is a form of drama, a genre of literature. But rarely do we read a screenplay before we see, or in lieu of seeing, a movie. Rarely would you study a screenplay in a literature class. A film is a series of 'moving talking pictures', which we must see and hear to understand and appreciate. Fortunately, DVD and CD players, iPods and even mobile phones make films as easy to watch as books are to read – which is one reason why the analysis and interpretation of film is so often an important component of introduction-to-literature classes.

The process of understanding, interpreting, analysing, and appreciating a film is, in some ways, more complex than the process of understanding written text. Viewing may be easier, more passive, or, to many, more fun than reading because a film packages for us the colour, motion, setting, and the special effects we must construct ourselves when we read a story. But film has a highly technical dimension, absent in poetry and fiction and present in a limited way in a live play. To really understand and appreciate a film, we need to consider these technical elements. Yes, we interpret a movie in the context of the standard elements of literature; we consider plot, theme, setting, character, point-of-view, imagery while we watch the film and after it has ended. But there are, as well, these technical elements we need to consider if we are to interpret and understand a film as completely as possible. Specifically, to understand and appreciate a film, we need some understanding of:

▶ how a director composes a 'shot'

▶ how a director positions and moves the camera

▶ how the film's editor chooses to assemble the shots into a coherent visual text.

The composition of the shot

Film is a series of still celluloid photographs or 'frames' flashed before us so quickly that they create an illusion of real-life movement and action. Most film reels travel at 24 frames per second (fps), so fast that our eye sees a movie the way it sees the real action and movement we experience in day-to-day life, though the movie is really the quintessential optical illusion.

Each frame is part of a shot. A shot is a single setting or moment of action in a film. A shot may be composed of a limited number of frames and thereby pass us by very quickly or it may be composed of thousands of frames and appear before us for some minutes. A director may try to compose a shot symmetrically by positioning props and characters of similar size and shape in similar positions on either side of the screen. Or she may stage an asymmetrical shot by placing props and actors of disproportionate size and number – but of equal visual significance – on either side of the screen. The 'equal visual significance' is crucial because a director wants balance and harmony even in an asymmetrical shot, unless, for artistic reasons, the director consciously seeks to establish a sense of imbalance. A shot ends when the camera 'cuts' to a different setting or moment of action – to the next shot. A shot must, at the very least, establish a setting, though sometimes, especially at the beginning of a film, that is all a shot does.

Within the film's narrative, shots become more complex, consisting of some kind of performance from an actor or from two or more actors in dialogue with each other. The actors move in ways appropriate to the film's purpose, their faces express their feelings and emotions, they speak, they use 'props', they dress in a way that indicates their role in the film.

Lighting is also an important element in the composition of a shot. Typically a shot is lit with *high key* or balanced lighting, which attempts to reproduce the natural, the real lighting we would expect within the given shot. But sometimes a director will toy with light to realise a particular artistic purpose. An especially brightly lit section of a shot filmed mainly with high key lighting will draw our attention to that part of the shot even if that part is not in the shot's foreground. *Low key* or *chiaroscuro* lighting darkens some aspects of a shot and can heighten fear and create suspense. *Fill light* might be used to eliminate shadows. *Backlighting* will highlight the edges of the actors and other elements within a shot, making those characters and elements more distinct. The main source of light in a shot is usually placed at eye level, but if it is placed above eye level (*top lighting*), it enhances actors' features; if it is placed below eye level (*under lighting*), it distorts features and makes characters appear rather ominous.

Shot size also influences the film's narrative and the viewers' response to it. An *extreme long shot* (ELS) is often used to establish setting, since an ELS can frame a large area – a complete cityscape, for example. An *extreme close up*, on the other hand, will focus attention on an important, specific detail – a guilty smirk, a phone about to ring, a wasp about to sting. In between are the more commonly used *long shot*, *mid shot*, and *close up*, their use dependent upon the director's narrative intent and on the level of audience attention he wishes to focus on particular details.

The duration of a shot or the *length of take* also influences tone and narrative flow. An average 'take' in a typical movie is about six seconds, but the duration tends to be longer at the beginning of a movie when the director is introducing to us the characters and establishing the settings within which they will interact. A serious dramatic film, slowly paced and with complex characters, will tend to have longer takes to accommodate the extended dialogue needed to establish character, motive, and plot. Action films are characterised by shorter takes, which augment the suspense and heighten the conflict typical of that genre.

The use of the camera

A film's director tells a story by focusing a camera on a person or a group of people; by following them around as they go to various places, do various things, and interact with various people; and by recording what they have to say. But the camera does not merely record the story; it influences the way filmgoers perceive, process, and understand the sequence of events which forms the movie's plot. Camera movement, angle, and depth of field are especially influential in shaping an audience's response to a film.

A camera can, for example, *pan* or rotate from left-to-right or right-to-left, perhaps to follow a moving object. Similarly, it can *track* a moving object, in which case the camera does more than pan, it moves along with the object upon which it is focusing. In a tracking shot, the camera is usually fitted to a dolly that runs on rails so the movement is steady, though a camera person might hold the camera if the director wants to create the reality effect that an unsteady shot can create. The recent invention of a contraption known as the *steadicam* allows for a compromise: a smoother movement with a hand-held camera. A camera can *tilt* or rotate up and down, a movement a director will often use to indicate height. If the director wants a big tilt combined with an option for horizontal movement, he or she will go with the versatile *crane shot*. In a *zoom* shot, the camera seems to move, sometimes quickly, sometimes slowly, toward an object upon which it wants to focus, 'seems to move' because it is really the camera lens that is changing position, not the camera itself.

Camera angle also influences perception. Usually, a director positions a camera at eye-level because that position corresponds to the audience's sense of reality. But the director might film from a *high camera angle* to establish a context for a scene or to indicate an imbalance of power between characters: a character photographed from above appears small and weak. Or the director might film from a *low camera angle* to highlight the fact that the person he or she is focusing on is large and powerful, perhaps somewhat ominous.

Depth of field refers to the visibility of characters and props in the foreground of a scene compared with the visibility of characters and props in the background of a scene. A *shallow focus shot* blurs images in the background to highlight character and action in the foreground. A *deep focus shot* allows the audience to see clearly what is behind the characters and props in the foreground. The choice depends upon narrative intent. If the director wants us to see something important going on behind the main action in the foreground, he or she will likely choose a deep focus shot.

Editing

Editing is the process of splicing together shots from a movie into a manner that is in keeping with the story-telling needs and intentions of the filmmaker. Usually shots are spliced together – i.e. edited – to form a coherent, chronological story, but a film editor, in collaboration with the director and producer, might splice shots together in a less-than-coherent or chronological manner to fulfil a variety of artistic purposes: to create suspense, to flashback to an earlier point in the story to establish character motivation, to juxtapose two separate stories against each other. One of the biggest responsibilities of a film editor is *continuity*. Filmgoers should not be conscious of an edit from one shot to another any more than they are conscious of the blinking of their eyes. An edit usually advances scene and plot sequentially, a process that helps make the edit seem invisible; but, even if the edit shifts direction of the movie markedly, the spatial, temporal, and narrative relationship of that edit to the previous one should be unobtrusive. In film making, one scene may be shot over the course of a few days, and the actors, from one day to the next, might inadvertently change clothes or wear jewellery they were not wearing earlier or change (even slightly) a hair style. The editor must watch for such changes so that an edit, within a scene that is supposed to take place at a given time and in a given place, does not reveal a change that could not have taken place. Some movie buffs take pride in spotting continuity errors and sharing them with others. Indeed, there are scores of websites devoted to pointing out continuity errors.

One common editing technique is the *shot/reverse shot edit*, often used when two characters are conversing. When one character speaks, the camera is on his or her face and shoulders, but the back of the other character's face and shoulders can also be seen. When that character responds, an edit is used to reverse the perspective so the attention of the viewers is focused on that character's words and on the facial expressions that accompany them. If the characters are not at eye level, if one character is sitting, for example, and the other standing, the editor needs to be aware of *eye-line match* and make sure, for example, that when the camera is focused on the sitting character, his or her eyes are looking up to the other character.

Frequently, a director will call for a *match on action* edit, which juxtaposes two or more different shots of one action, one filmed from a different angle than the other, perhaps, or from a different distance or perspective. An orchestra conductor might, for example, be filmed from the back so the director can illustrate the musicians' perspective and responses, then be filmed from the front to get the audience's reaction, then from the side to indicate the stage manager's response to the performance. The director might even cut to the exterior of the concert hall while the orchestra continues to perform to show, for example, a group of terrorists creeping toward the building to kidnap a cabinet minister when she exits. This type of edit is called a *cutaway shot*.

A similar editing technique is the *cross-cut*, in which two (perhaps more) different but related actions are juxtaposed with each other several times. Suppose, for example, that while the terrorists race away with the cabinet minister, the director cuts to the police visiting the minister's office, where they are told that she is at the concert; then he cuts back to the terrorists as they race the cabinet minister to the plane, taking her out of the country; then he cuts back to the police racing to catch up with the kidnappers before they reach the plane. Cross-cuts are frequently used to heighten suspense.

The *180 degree rule* is another important principle of film editing. The rule asserts that the camera should not cross an imaginary line running through the middle of the action, especially if that action involves two or more characters. Suppose, for example, that Tom and Harry are confronting each other and that the camera is to Tom's left and, therefore, to Harry's right. In the course of the scene, the director should not cut a shot, then move the camera across the line to film from that perspective. Now the camera would be to Tom's right and Harry's left, and the effect can be disorienting to viewers. As with all rules, of course, some directors deliberately break the 180 degree rule to achieve a particular effect.

The *30 degree rule* asserts that when two shots of one action in one location are edited together, the camera should, for the second of these shots, move position by at least 30 degrees. If it does not, the edit is obtrusive because it seems that the action does not change perspective so much as jump out of focus; indeed, such an edit is called a *jump cut*. Sometimes, to avoid a jump cut, or to create a particular effect, an editor might end a shot not by immediately cutting to another shot but by *fading* the shot to black and fading the next shot from black. Or a shot can appear to *dissolve* into the next shot or can appear to be *wiped* off the screen while the next shot gradually emerges.

These rules and conventions of editing, then, help establish the continuity the audience expects so they can follow the film's narrative faithfully. A good film editor creates the illusion that his job does not exist, that it is life the audience is watching unfold before them, not images on strips of celluloid carefully spliced together.

Some film directors, however, want to stress that film need not always hold a mirror up to life, that film can, instead, shatter mirrors and thereby sacrifice narrative to make social or political statements. To help them achieve these goals, these directors often use a technique known as *discontinuity editing*. In such films, the cuts or edits are obvious and sometimes jarring. The best know type of discontinuity editing is *montage*, a series of brief, sometimes instantaneous, shots spliced together, used not necessarily to advance the narrative but often to kick start the audience's attention in certain desired directions. Montage can intensify the violence of war, the horror of a murder, the tenderness of love. The *freeze frame* also creates discontinuity because, in reality, a moving image cannot suddenly stop as if frozen in mid-stride or in mid-air. But the freeze frame is a good editing technique to use when a director wants to highlight, to focus viewer attention on a single image.

Let's look now at three highly-regarded films and analyse them, focusing on those technical aspects discussed above, those technical aspects that distinguish films from other literary genres.

The Third Man, directed by Carol Reed

Carol Reed's 1949 movie *The Third Man* illustrates how cinematic style and technology can add texture to a story in ways an artist working in print cannot.

The Third Man is set in Vienna after the Second World War. Vienna is a shadow of its former sophisticated self, a bleak city of bombed-out buildings, incompetently and corruptly administered by a consortium of British, Russian, American, and French bureaucrats. Harry Lime (played by Orson Welles) runs a medical unit in the city and has invited an old friend, Holly Martins (played by Joseph Cotton), to come and work for him, as a glorified secretary. But Martins learns, right after he arrives in Vienna, that Lime has died after being run over by a truck. Martins senses suspicious circumstances surrounding his friend's death and launches his own investigation. This suspicion intensifies when he is threatened by some of Lime's acquaintances and after a porter, who had witnessed Lime's death and who was going to provide Martins with some crucial information – specifically that there was a mysterious third man at the scene of Lime's death – is murdered. Ultimately, Martins learns that Lime is alive but staged his own death – by murdering one of his own accomplices – to escape from the authorities, who want him for selling diluted penicillin on the black market. Horrified by his friend's crimes and disillusioned by the general corruption he witnesses in Vienna, Martins helps the authorities track Lime down. Indeed, it is Martins himself who ends up shooting Lime as he tries to escape underground through the sewers of Vienna.

Stylistically, *The Third Man* owes much to the influence of the *film noir* genre. In the early 1940s, a series of films featuring amoral characters cheating, murdering, or double-crossing each other in seedy, dingy alleys and apartments were produced. The atmosphere in film noir movies is always bleak and dreary. These films were deliberately poorly lit and most of the action occurs at night, action which often features violent scenes, shot from obscure camera angles. The sharply-edited, climatic chase scene in *The Third Man*, through the sewers of Vienna, where the armed and morally bankrupt Harry Lime seeks escape from the police is typical film noir action. The camera, often weirdly angled, pans the ancient tunnel walls and fetid cobblestone walkways, pursuing Harry as he runs up a circular stairway and tries to push a manhole cover open to reach the street and continue his escape. All the while, the refrains of a lone zither are heard, creating a memorable score that augments the film noir ambience.

The *femme fatale* is another staple of film noir, and, in *The Third Man*, this role is played by Alida Valli, who is Harry's lover, Anna Schmidt. Holly is bewitched by Anna whom he meets while he investigates his friend's death. Martins tries to rescue Anna who, as a Czech, must turn herself in to the Russian sector. But Anna is furious with Martins when she learns he is helping authorities capture a man she still loves, and she refuses his help. As the movie comes to an end, Martins is seen waiting for Anna, after Lime's funeral. She approaches slowly; the camera holds her a very long stationary shot; then she walks deliberately by, without a word, a gesture, a look.

Another cinematically effective sequence in *The Third Man* occurs when Major Calloway, the British military police officer (played by Trevor Howard), who is hunting down Harry Lime, tries to convince Martins that his friend is a wanted criminal. Calloway shows Martins the evidence: fingerprints, photographs of accomplices, vials of stolen penicillin. The evidence is presented in a striking montage sequence, which gradually and dramatically convinces Martins that Lime has, indeed, become a truly evil man.

Martins is devastated, goes out drinking, and pays a visit to Anna. Anna's cat is frightened and runs off. The camera then dramatically moves among the plants on Anna's window sill, then moves out the window to the dark, wet street below. It finds the cat and tracks it as it creeps its way to a doorway, where a man's foot is visible. Meanwhile, Martins, rebuffed by Anna, leaves the apartment, hears the meow of Anna's cat, and sees the man's foot. Martins challenges the man. A neighbour, irritated by the noise, turns on his light, which illuminates the smirking face of Harry Lime. The sudden reappearance of a character thought dead is a common cinematic trope, and informed viewers may not be shocked by Harry's reappearance. But in few other movies is this trope handled so deftly and effectively as it is in *The Third Man*. The *film noir* ambience of the scene, combined with the chiaroscuro lighting, illuminating Harry Lime's face, with its self-satisfied almost coquettish expression, creates one of the most startling and memorable resurrection moments in film history.

Harry flees, but Martins contacts Harry's co-conspirators and arranges a meeting. The meeting takes place on a Ferris wheel, in a scene that has become part of film legend. A microcosm of Vienna, indeed, of all of post-war Europe, the Ferris wheel is all that is left of a once-bustling amusement park. War has ravaged Vienna; few things work; and so many of the children who would play in the park are hospitalised, victims of the violence of war. As the Ferris wheel rises, Martins confronts Lime, asking him if he has ever seen the victims of his crimes: the sick children who cannot get penicillin because Lime waters it down and sells it to the highest bidders. Harry's response is cynical and contemptuous, as he suggests his childhood friend would do the same if he had the chance to make a lot of money. At the top of the ride, he threatens to kill Martins but reconsiders when he learns that the authorities know Lime is still alive. But he continues his twisted and perverted rant, arguing that societies governed through terror and corruption – societies like Italy under the Borgias – produced Michelangelo and Leonardo da Vinci, while societies ruled with peace, democracy, and brotherhood – countries like Switzerland – have produced only the cuckoo clock.

Still Martins is reluctant to turn Lime in but agrees to do so, when Major Calloway promises he will not turn Anna over to the Russians. When Anna refuses to be a part of a conspiracy to capture a man she still loves, Calloway takes Martins on a tour of a children's hospital where they see the victims of Lime's scam. Martins agrees to help capture his erstwhile friend, in fact he kills his friend in the climatic chase sequence.

The Graduate, directed by Mike Nichols
Released in 1967, *The Graduate* is the story of Benjamin Braddock (Dustin Hoffman), a young man who returns home to Los Angeles, after graduating from an Eastern Ivy League school, to try to decide what he is going to do for the rest of his life. The very concept of the future oppresses him, and so, instead of trying to make any decisions, Ben sits around the pool all day, doing as little as possible, despite a family friend's now famous recommendation that Ben get in to 'plastics.' Plastics, of course, the plastic culture of American materialism and superficial contentment – embodied by his parents – is exactly what Ben does *not* want to get in to.

After a party at Ben's parents' house, Mrs Robinson (Anne Bancroft), the wife of Ben's father's law partner, asks Ben to drive her home then attempts to seduce him. He resists at first but, bored and lethargic, he eventually bumbles his way into an affair with the seductively beautiful, manipulative, and controlling Mrs Robinson. When the Robinson's daughter Elaine (Katherine Ross) comes back from Berkeley, Ben's parents insist Ben ask her out, and Ben can't raise suspicions by refusing to do so and agrees, despite the frantically maniacal protests from Mrs Robinson. The children fall for each other, but Elaine furiously refuses to see him ever again, after she finds out Ben has had an affair with her mother. But she has become Ben's happily-ever-after, and he stalks her, following her to Berkeley, conspiring to see her. He is encouraged when she visits him, even though it is to tell him she is marrying someone else, and, eventually, he tracks her to Santa Barbara on her wedding day. He arrives just after she has exchanged vows, but she responds to his shouts, and he drags her out of the church. As the movie comes to an end, they are escaping together on a city bus.

The Graduate reveals the extent to which the technology of film – camera movement, cutting, shot composition – can move forward a story and add layers of meaning to it. For example, after Ben escapes the clutches of Mrs Robinson, the first time she tries to seduce him, he runs downstairs where Mr Robinson is pouring himself a drink. He begins to engage the terrified Ben in conversation. Director Mike Nichols films the scene with a shallow field of focus, so when Mrs Robinson floats down the stairs behind the men, she is blurred, insignificant, the way her husband literally sees her. Yet she is physically above the two men and so, in an important symbolic sense, more significant, more powerful than they. She is, after all, about to cuckold her husband and she will have her way with the attractive young man who has caught her eye.

In another sequence, Ben is swimming in his family pool. As he lunges his body onto his air mattress, a quick, brilliant edit shows him lunging at Mrs Robinson, about to make love to her, as she lies prone and naked in bed. The camera plays between the two scenes, at times making it seem as if Ben and Mrs Robinson's secret affair is taking place not at a hotel but in a room in Ben's house, next to the room where his parents are calmly eating their breakfast. The sequence suggests that Ben equates his relationship with Mrs Robinson with a cool swim in his pool and values it about as much, and suggests, as well, his growing power in the relationship, which he will eventually have the audacity – engendered by his love for Elaine – to end.

The Graduate is also justly famous for its range of shots, from extreme long, to close up. In the movie's last sequence, for example, the camera follows Ben as he races to Santa Barbara to stop Elaine's wedding. An extreme long shot follows Ben's sports car as it tears down the highway and crosses the bridge into Santa Barbara, then cuts to mid-shots and close ups as he arrives at a gas station where he frantically tears at a phone book, trying to find out where the wedding is taking place – and forgetting to buy gas. He runs out of gas and has to run the rest of the way to the church. The camera soars skyward again, making it seem like Ben is making slow progress towards his goal. But he gets to the church, makes his way to the loft, pounds on the window, and shouts Elaine's name. The camera zooms in to a series of close-ups on characters' faces, Elaine's hopeful, Mr and Mrs Robinson's twisted with rage. The sequence is a microcosm of the movie itself, showing as it does Ben's frantic struggle to make some meaning of his life, Mrs Robinson's deadly combination of hysteria and despair, Mr Robinson's malice, and Elaine's cry for help, as she realises it is Ben who is her soul mate.

Finally, *The Graduate* is enriched by the songs of Simon and Garfunkle, which augment the film's themes and the many moods of its characters. 'The Sounds of Silence' echoes Ben's despair, his soul's silence, which like a cancer will grow, unless he takes control of his life. 'April, Come She Will' and 'Scarborough Fair' suggest Ben's romantic streak, his hope that love will redeem him. Paul Simon wrote one song, 'Mrs Robinson', especially for the movie and perfectly captured the anguish of this middle-aged woman who has lost her faith in her childhood heroes like Joe DiMaggio; who is cynical about politicians' promises, convinced now that 'when you've got to choose/Any way you look at it you lose'; and who is blind to the promise that Jesus, at least, 'loves you more than you will know'.

Fargo, produced and directed by Joel and Ethan Cohen

The Coen brothers, Joel and Ethan's, 1996 film *Fargo* takes its title from a North Dakota town but is actually set mainly in and around Brainerd, Minnesota.

It is the story of a car salesman, Jerry Lundegaard (William H. Macy), who devises a twisted plan to raise the money he needs to get out of debt and finance a business venture. He will hire a couple of thugs – Carl Showalter (Steve Buscemi) and Gaear Grimsrud (Peter Stormare) – to kidnap his wife, hit up his rich father-in-law for a million dollar ransom, pay a fraction of the money out to the kidnappers, and pocket the rest. But as soon as the plan begins to be executed, it becomes a complete debacle. The crime turns in to a triple homicide when the kidnappers are pulled over by a state trooper. They kill the trooper and the innocent couple who happen to drive by and witness the crime. Jerry's overbearing, meddlesome father-in-law insists on delivering the ransom himself and is shot and killed by Showalter, who buries most of the million dollar ransom money in the snow, before returning to the lake house where his partner is waiting for him. The partner has since shot dead Jerry's wife, their kidnap victim, because she would not stop whining. Showalter pays Grimsrud his $40,000 share, saying nothing about the $900,000 windfall he has hidden. But when he insists on keeping the new car that Jerry gave them as part of the deal, Grimsrud chops him up with an axe and attempts to dispose of the body with the help of a wood chipper.

Meanwhile, Police Chief Marge Gunderson (Frances McDormand) has begun her investigation of the triple homicide. Even though she is seven months pregnant, she methodically tracks down the kidnappers, and establishes Lundegaard's guilt. Her investigation leads her to Jerry's car lot, where she patiently begins to put pieces of the puzzle together. She tracks the kidnappers down just as Grimsrud is feeding his partner's body to the wood chipper. Later, Jerry is captured in a motel, trying to make his escape.

Cinematically, the film is notable for the blizzard scenes, one at the beginning of the movie, the other near the end. As *Fargo* opens a white screen gradually acquires some texture, as car lights appear, and we realize we are watching not a white screen but a highway in a blizzard. The car is being driven by Jerry Lundegaard, and he is pulling a trailer on which rides the tan sienna automobile, which he is delivering to the kidnappers in Fargo (the only time the town appears in the film) as part of their payment for kidnapping his wife. The cold, bleak, unforgiving setting intensifies the sense that the action of the film is occurring within a moral vacuum, soon evident as a husband meets with two criminals, one a psychopathic killer, to arrange for the kidnapping of his wife. The ineptitude of all involved undercuts the violence with humour but never redeems their evil.

Near the end of the movie another car gradually emerges from and takes shape amidst a forbidding blizzard. This time the car is being driven by Marge Gunderson and in the back seat is her prisoner, Grimsrud. She lectures him about his horrific crimes, concluding by noting 'and it's a beautiful day'. Her words are genuine, not ironic; for Marge represents all that is good and warm, all that can cope with the cold, indeed see beauty in it, and that can transcend the perfidy of the kidnappers, that can restore order and harmony to what seemed to have become a nihilistic world. She treats everyone with kindness and respect, but when her sense of justice is challenged, she becomes the tough cop, the relentless detective. Seven months pregnant, she has no qualms about bringing new life into her world; indeed, the last scene shows her and her husband, wholly in love and at peace with each other, yearning for the two months to pass so they can welcome new life. Outside, a blizzard may be raging and murderers may be stalking their next victims, but with new life forming within her and a loving husband next to her, Marge represents the triumph of the human spirit that can crush the Jerry Lundegaards and Gaear Grimsruds and still perceive, in the midst of a blizzard, real and metaphorical, a beautiful day.

In another notable scene, a long high angle shot displays a single vehicle on the snow-covered roof of a parking lot. The car belongs to Jerry, who appears after he has left a meeting with his father-in-law, where he has been demeaned and humiliated. The camera zooms in to show Jerry scraping frost of his windshield. Suddenly, he becomes conscious of the pathetic turn his life has taken, of the consequences of his recent actions, and, in a fit of rage and frustration, he begins to scrape maniacally at his windshield. But congenitally inept, mild-manner, and ineffectual, he soon calms down and methodically scrapes the snow off his windshield. Later, on the roof of another otherwise deserted parking lot, his father-in-law is shot dead when he challenges one of his daughter's kidnappers.

Tutorial

Progress questions

1. Explain how a film differs from a play.

2. How can lighting influence the way we view and interpret a film?

3. How does camera angle influence the way we view and interpret a film?

4. What is the role of the film editor?

Seminar discussion
1. What criteria do your think the members of BAFTA consider when they select the films for the best-film-of-the-year award?

2. What elements do you think a film needs to make it a success?

3. Why are some films panned by the critics but loved by the general audience and others praised by the critics but are failures at the box office?

Practical assignment
Select one of the films nominated for last year's or this year's BAFTA Award or Academy Award for best picture. Go online and find five reviews of this film. Write a report of approximately 1,000 words, in which you analyse and synthesize the content of these reviews.

Study and revision tip
When you view a film, consider how its technical aspects – shot composition, camera angle and distance, and editing – contribute to the overall effect it has on the audience.

6

Understanding the Sequence of Events

One-minute overview – A story, a narrative poem and a play are made up of a sequence of events. These events, the order in which they occur, and the relationship of the events to each other, comprise the **plot** of the literary work. Writers usually present their plots in the temporal order in which the events occurred. This is known as a **sequential plot**. Sometimes authors will choose not to narrate the events in chronological order but will alter the time order to create suspense. Such a story has a **non-sequential plot**. A story that has a sequence of events familiar to readers because they have read or been told similar stories before has an **archetypal plot**. Writers (and readers) tend to prefer plots that are unpredictable. The surprise ending or the **plot twist** is a time-honoured plot device. Events in a story will often unfold in a way opposite to the way we had expected they would. Such a story is said to have an **ironic plot**. In this chapter we will explore the:

- ► sequential plot
- ► non-sequential plot
- ► archetypal plot
- ► plot twist
- ► plot and irony.

The sequential plot

Life is a temporal sequence of events, so stories, which mirror life, are generally narrated chronologically, that is in the order in which those events occur in time. Those events, their relationship to each other, and the order in which they are presented to the reader comprise the **plot** of a story, a play or a narrative poem. A **sequential plot** is one in which the events are narrated in the order in which they occurred in time.

Example

Katherine Mansfield, 'The Garden Party'

Katherine Mansfield's classic story 'The Garden Party', for example, begins on a fine summer morning and ends the evening of that same day. In between, the events which form the plot of the story occur.

The well-to-do Sheridan family makes plans for an elaborate garden party to be held at their beautiful New Zealand home. They learn about the death of a neighbour, a young carter, killed when his horse shied at a tractor and threw its rider. A working man, the young carter lived in one of the row of poor cottages below the Sheridan's mansion.

Laura, the only member of the Sheridan family who has anything of a social conscience, insists they cancel the party. Other members of her family can't imagine doing anything so extreme simply because a mere workman has died. Laura, too, relents when she sees how dazzling she looks in her new hat and how exciting it will be to show her beauty off to the garden party guests. When the party is over, she takes a basket of sandwiches, left over from the party, to the widow and children of the dead man. Against her will, she is led into the room where the dead carter lies. She can think of only three words to say, 'Forgive my hat'. The words suggest that Laura's social conscience, implied earlier in the story, will continue to flourish.

The non-sequential plot

While most stories are narrated in a chronological sequence, some authors will choose to hold back an important incident that occurred before the chronological ending of the story. In other words, the story will have a **non-sequential plot**. The advantage of a non-sequential plot is **suspense.** The author holds back an event because the plot of the story turns on that event. To reveal it earlier would diminish the story's impact, while to reveal it at the end, or out of chronological sequence, keeps the reader engaged in the story's plot. The technique of narrating an event which occurred before the point in the story to which the narrator has advanced is known as a **flashback**.

Example

William Faulkner, 'A Rose for Emily'

One of the most frequently taught stories with a non-sequential plot is William Faulkner's 'A Rose for Emily'. Chronologically, the events in the story occur as follows. Emily Grierson is a young southern belle who falls on hard times when her father dies in 1894. Some years later, she meets Homer Baron, a Northerner, who has come to the town of Jefferson to pave the sidewalks. They date for a period of time, and the townspeople think they will marry. Emily visits the pharmacist and buys some arsenic. Homer disappears. Some townspeople complain about a noxious odour emanating from Emily's house. The years pass. For a while, Emily teaches little girls how to paint pictures onto china. More years pass, and Emily becomes more and more reclusive. She refuses to allow the town authorities to attach a number to her house to help the postman deliver mail. She refuses to pay taxes. By now in her seventies, she chases away a group of town councillors who come to her house to collect her back taxes. She tells them to talk to Colonel Sartoris, the mayor of Jefferson, and he will explain everything to them. Sartoris was the mayor before Emily even knew Homer and is long-since dead. Finally, at the age of seventy-four, Emily dies. Townspeople find the remains of Homer's body in her bedroom. A strand of grey hair on the pillow indicates that Emily continued to lie with Homer long after she poisoned him.

Faulkner deliberately alters the chronological order of the events in the story. He begins by telling of the death of Emily, then flashes way back to 1894 when Mayor Sartoris remitted the Grierson taxes. Then he moves forward, describing the visit from the aldermen. Next, he describes the complaint about the smell, then he flashes way back again to describe the death of Emily's father. He then moves forward again to describe the courtship of Emily and Homer, Emily's purchase of the arsenic, and the disappearance of Homer. The story comes full circle as the author again describes Emily's death. It ends with the discovery of Homer's body and the evidence of Emily's necrophilia.

Faulkner narrates his story out of chronological order for two reasons. First, the technique increases the suspense in what is, in a sense, a murder mystery. Second the lack of chronological sequence reflects the main character's insanity – her own inability to cope with, even understand, the passing of time.

The archetypal plot

An archetypal plot is a sequence of events forming a type of story which has recurred throughout the history of a civilisation and which is, consequently, shared by all members of that civilisation. The psychologist Carl Jung argued that an archetype is part of our subconscious heritage, and that we share such stories on a subconscious level.

▶ The 'battle between good and evil' is an example of an archetypal plot which runs through our culture from Homer through Milton to *Star Wars*.

▶ The 'quest' is another example of an archetypal plot. It is manifested in such stories as Jason and the Argonaut's quest for the golden fleece and the many stories whose plots revolve around the search for the Holy Grail (the communal cup Christ used at the Last Supper).

Example of an archetypal 'rescue' plot
Joseph Conrad, 'Heart of Darkness'
The rescue is another example of an archetypal plot. Typically, the rescue archetype involves a hero overcoming a villain to rescue a damsel in distress. Joseph Conrad's novella *Heart of Darkness* is also an example of the rescue archetype, but under a different set of circumstances. It is the story of an unemployed English sailor, Charlie Marlow, who is commissioned by a major trading company to sail into the heart of Africa and bring home one of the company's agents, Kurtz. At one time, Kurtz had been a most successful ivory merchant, but something has happened to him, and the company, desperate to protect its economic interests, needs to find out what. Marlow endures punishing journeys at sea and on land. His patience is tested when he must wait for months for his steamer to

be repaired. He witnesses the inhuman treatment of the African people who are no more than slaves for European companies exploiting Africa's riches, its ivory specifically.

Finally, he reaches Kurtz. Kurtz had come to Africa, not only to strike it rich but also as a humanitarian determined to improve conditions among the exploited African people. But he, too, is corrupted by the chance for immense wealth and power. He harvests all of the ivory he can find, and ultimately establishes himself as the leader of the African people among whom he lives. He is emotionally, mentally and physically exhausted when Marlow manages finally to rescue him (against his will) and sneak him on board. He dies on board, but not before he realises what he had become, not before he repents – with the much-quoted line, 'The horror, the horror' – the loss of his humanity which has been corrupted by the greed and exploitation which characterise European imperialism.

Heart of Darkness is an archetypal rescue story. It is also Conrad's indictment of European imperialism. It is also a quest and includes, even, the descent into the underworld which is an archetypal element of the quest legend. Marlow's journey to the heart of the dark continent is his own symbolic journey to enlightenment. He is, in fact, compared to a Buddha several times throughout the story. Through his contact with the ivory traders, he learns the truth about the European mission in Africa. The adjectives 'civilised' to describe Europe and 'uncivilised' to describe Africa are used, ironically, several times throughout the story. Through his contact with Kurtz, he learns that power can corrupt even good men; that, given a certain set of circumstances, especially the opportunity for enormous wealth and power, we might forget about our values and ideals.

It is significant that Marlow tells his tale to a lawyer, an accountant and a company director. They represent the Establishment, men who need to learn the lessons Marlow learned through his literal and psychological descent into the heart of darkness.

The plot twist

Readers do not like predictable plots, so writers will often twist their plot away from the direction in which it appears to be heading. A character will die unexpectedly or a secret will be revealed or an innocent-looking character will be revealed as the guilty party, and, as a result, the plot will strike out in a whole new direction.

Example

James Thurber, 'The Catbird Seat'
In Thurber's story 'The Catbird Seat' a mild-mannered file clerk, Mr Martin, resolves to murder a supervisor, Mrs Ulgine Barrows, who is threatening to re-structure his precious department. Late one night he shows up at the supervisor's flat, determined to do her in. But as he converses with his victim a whole new idea begins to blossom and the plot of the story twists away from the direction in which it seems to be heading.

To Mrs Barrows' utter amazement, Mr Martin, who is famous at work for his abstemious habits and modest lifestyle, accepts a drink and a smoke. Then, to Mrs Barrows' continued amazement, he refers to their boss, Mr Fitweiler, as a 'windbag' and 'an old goat' and claims he is going to murder him when he is 'coked to the gills' on heroin.

Next day, Mrs Barrows reports the incident to Mr Fitweiler. Fitweiler calls Martin in and asks him if he visited Mrs Barrows last night and made all kinds of threats. Martin appears stunned and denies everything. Mr Fitweiler sends for the men in white coats who haul Mrs Barrows, kicking and screaming, away, while Martin returns to his beloved files, 'wearing a look of studious concentration'.

Plot and irony

Irony is the distance between what is supposed to happen and what really does happen. For example, it is ironic when

▶ a Chief of Police is convicted of a crime
▶ a heart specialist has a heart attack
▶ a professional writer makes a 'speling eror'.

In literature, drama especially, irony – known as **dramatic irony** – can exert a powerful influence on plot. The audience at a play squirms when a character says something he or she believes to be true but the audience knows to be false. Shakespeare's Othello, for example, is always praising Iago for his loyalty. The audience knows Iago is systematically plotting Othello's downfall behind Othello's back. The irony of Othello's praise intensifies the audience's interest in the plot's development and outcome.

Example
Thomas Hardy, 'The Ruined Maid'
In his poem, 'The Ruined Maid', Hardy uses irony to defuse the myth of the superiority of the simple country life over the wicked temptations of the city. A young farm worker, on a visit to the city, sees an old friend. The farm girl had been told that this friend, Amelia, had succumbed to the temptations of the city, been forced into prostitution, and was now a broken, a 'ruined maid'. Amelia, however, is nothing of the kind. In fact, she is beautifully dressed, the picture of health, well-spoken, and content. Her responses to her friend's question resonate with irony. When the farm girl comments on Amelia's improved speech, Amelia comments, 'Some polish is gained with one's ruin' (line 12). The ultimate irony comes, in the last stanza of Hardy's six-stanza poem, when the farm girl expresses her wish to be just like her old friend. Note the anapaestic rhythm (see Chapter 3) of the lines:

> 'I wish I had feathers, a fine sweeping gown,
> And a delicate face, and could strut about Town!'
> "My dear – a raw country girl, such as you be,
> Cannot quite expect that. You ain't ruined," said she.'
>   (lines 21–24).

Tutorial

Progress questions
1. What is an archetype? List five examples of what you would consider to be an archetypal plot.

2. What is meant by a sequential plot? A non-sequential plot?

3. Why would a writer choose to narrate his or her story out of its chronological sequence?

4. How might irony influence plot?

Seminar discussion

1. Why are flashbacks and plot twists so often features of detective stories?

2. Why is irony such a powerful tool for a dramatist?

3. The plot of a story can be based on current social issues. Discuss some stories you are familiar with, the plots of which address social issues.

Practical assignment

Write a brief account of what you did yesterday. Rewrite your story using a flashback or otherwise altering the temporal order of events. Rewrite it again with an invented plot twist.

Study and revision tip

When you read a story, a narrative poem or a play, note down each of the major events which occurs. Consider the order in which the author presents the events, and his or her reasons for ordering events in that way.

7

Observing the Characters

One-minute overview – We respond to the characters in literature on a more familiar level than we do to other literary elements. We tend to **identify** with a fictitious character, comparing the character's values, ideals, actions, goals, appearance and personality with our own. This identification adds interest to the plot of the story (the subject of Chapter 6) and depth to the theme (see Chapter 10). A character might change as a result of the experience he or she undergoes throughout the story or miss the opportunity to change. A character who does change as a result of experience is known as a **dynamic** character; a character who does not is known as a **static** character. A **stereotypical** character is a person identified by one dominant trait, such as vanity, sloth or greed. A character's actions can illustrate the **irony** of life. A writer can poke fun or **satirise** society through the actions of his or her characters. In this chapter we will explore:

▶ dynamic characters
▶ static characters
▶ stereotypical characters
▶ character and irony
▶ character and satire.

Dynamic characters

A **dynamic** character, sometimes referred to as a **round** character, is one whose values, attitudes and/or ideals change as a result of the experience the character undergoes throughout the story. In Chapter 2, we met Napoleon, the main character of Frank O'Connor's story, 'Guests of the Nation', and noted how the execution of two British soldiers changed his perception of the war.

In Chapter 6, we met Laura Sheridan whose attitude towards the social structure of her community changes as a result of her brief experience with the family of the dead carter. Napoleon and Laura are examples of dynamic characters.

Example

D. H. Lawrence, 'The Odour of Chrysanthemums'

Elizabeth Bates, the main character in Lawrence's story 'The Odour of Chrysanthemums', changes as a result of a tragic experience around which the story's plot revolves. Elizabeth is an educated and intelligent woman married to a Nottingham miner and bitter because her marriage is not working out. She is exasperated by her humble lifestyle and constantly angry at her hard-drinking husband. On the night the story is set, her husband is late yet again for dinner, and Elizabeth thinks he has gone to the pub. But as the evening advances and he still does not return, she begins to worry.

The odour of chrysanthemums foreshadows a significant event. Elizabeth's daughter Annie loves the chrysanthemums Elizabeth has in the pocket of her apron and tells her mother how beautiful they are. Elizabeth replies they are not beautiful to her because she associates them with her marriage, the birth of her children, and the first time Walter was brought home drunk, because he had a chrysanthemum in his buttonhole.

Her fears are confirmed when she learns there has been an accident at the mine and Walter has suffocated. There is some evidence to suggest the 'accident' was, in fact, a suicide. The doctor notes that Walter's body was not crushed; the mine manager says 'seems as it was done on purpose'.

Consciously, Elizabeth does not respond to this possibility, but subconsciously, as she cleans her husband's body, she begins to realise she was not the only one unhappy in the marriage, that Walter's guilt over his inability to make her happy might have contributed to his drinking and possibly to the 'accident' as well. Elizabeth moves beyond herself and her own disappointment and begins to see their life together from her late husband's point of view. She realises, with shame, that she 'had denied him as himself'. She failed to accept her husband for what he was, he sensed her disappoint, and was, himself, unhappy.

Lawrence believed marriage should be a 'mutual unison in separateness'. The insight which makes Elizabeth so dynamic a character is her realisation that, consumed as she was by her own bitterness and disappointment, she failed to acknowledge her husband's despair over his inability to make her happy. She failed to give him a chance, failed to acknowledge his own separateness.

Static characters

A static character, also known as a **flat** character, is one who is offered the chance for positive change but who, for one reason or another, fails to embrace it. The character might be too afraid to change. He or she might be naïve and not realise there is a need to change. The character might be too proud to change in a way which might inconvenience him or her, even while it might benefit someone else.

Example
T. S. Eliot, 'The Love Song of J. Alfred Prufrock'
Eliot's Prufrock is a typical static character. He doesn't like who he is, and he wants to change. He is a middle-aged man who would like to have a serious relationship with a woman but who is too insecure to ask the woman the 'overwhelming question' which would lead to such a relationship.

Throughout his dramatic monologue, Prufrock speculates on the kind of man he would like to be. He would like to be a romantic figure like the artist Michelangelo whom women talk about. He would like to be heroic, like John the Baptist, miraculous like Lazarus, or the leader that Hamlet finally becomes. He would like to ask the woman to marry him, perhaps, or perhaps simply to like and respect him enough to at least consider a more serious relationship.

But he is obsessed with his bald head and skinny arms; worried that his clothes are not right; convinced he lacks a winning personality. His most pronounced concern is a fear of rejection, a fear that if he bears his soul to this woman, she will proclaim her lack of interest, thereby completely shattering his already fragile self-esteem. And so he does nothing. He expresses his desire to change his image, dress more stylishly, assert himself more, but he is stuck in his conservative middle-aged rut.

And so the poem ends as it began. Prufrock is convinced the mermaids will not sing for him. He is, metaphorically, drowned by his inability to relate to others the way he would like to. He is static, and he seems incapable of becoming the man he would like to be.

Stereotypical characters

A stereotypical character is one who can be identified by a single dominant trait. In our discussion of comedy in Chapter 4, we noted that stereotypical characters are often sources of humour, though it is a humour sometimes tinged with racism and sexism in stereotypes such as the blond bimbo or the parsimonious Scot. Stereotypes are also associated with various professions: the absent-minded professor, the scruffy artist, the dumb jock are all stereotypical characters.

Example

Robert Browning, 'My Last Duchess'

Robert Browning's classic poem, 'My Last Duchess', is a dramatic monologue (see Chapter 3), narrated by an Italian duke. He addresses an ambassador from the court of the Count of Tyrol, whose daughter the Duke wants to marry. He shows off a portrait of his former wife, his last duchess, and, in the process, tells the ambassador about her. He has an ulterior motive in doing so. He does not want the count's daughter to make the same mistakes his last duchess made and meet the same fate she met.

The Duke comes across as a man obsessed with his own self-importance, a man who insists his social inferiors, among whom he includes his wife, pay due deference to him and his 'nine-hundred-years-old name' (line 33). His last duchess, it appears, was not sufficiently in awe of him. She flirts with other men and treats her husband like an ordinary man. He refuses to talk to his wife and explain his concerns to her because he feels it would be a sign of weakness, 'and I chuse/Never to stoop' (lines 42–43). And so he has her murdered:

... I gave commands;
Then all smiles stopped together...
    (lines 45–46)

He tells all this to the count's ambassador so the count's daughter will know the proper way to behave in so august a presence.

The Duke is a stereotypical arrogant aristocrat. He insists that people beneath him act the way he expects them to act. If they do not, they are disposed of unceremoniously. Like many stereotypical characters, however, his dominant trait might mask an even stronger trait which lurks beneath his overt personality. Many readers sense some fear and insecurity beneath the Duke's arrogance and vanity.

Character and irony

In our discussion of plot, in Chapter 6 , we defined **irony** as the distance between what is supposed to happen and what actually does happen. In literature, a character's actions are ironic if that character behaves in a way which is at odds with the way that person appears to be. We expect the vicar will be righteous, so we say it is ironic when he is found in bed with the bishop's wife. Indeed, in literature, irony and hypocrisy are often bedfellows.

Example
Edwin Arlington Robinson, 'Richard Cory'
Robinson's character, Richard Cory, is a man who seems to have everything going for him. He is rich, good looking, and widely respected. Ordinary people who live in his community look at Richard Cory and wish they could be like him. The irony is that, despite superficial appearances, Richard is desperately unhappy, as the ending of the poem makes clear:

So on we worked, and waited for the light,
And went without the meat, and cursed the bread;
And Richard Cory, one calm summer night,
Went home and put a bullet through his head.
    (lines 13–16)

Character and satire

Satire is a literary form through which a writer pokes fun at those aspects of his society, especially those people and those social institutions which the author thinks are corrupt and in need of change. There are two types of satire, Horatian satire and Juvenalian satire.

Horatian satire

Named after the Roman poet, Horace, this is a relatively gentle type of satire in which the author uses humour to make us laugh at people who are vain and hypocritical, and at social conditions which need reform. Pope's well-known mock-epic poem, *The Rape of the Lock*, is an example of Horatian satire, wherein Pope makes fun of a group of rich self-absorbed young people.

Juvenalian satire

Named after the Roman poet, Juvenal, this form of satire uses bitter sarcasm more than humour and, indeed, is often tinged with cruelty. Alexander Pope's friend, Jonathan Swift, favoured Juvenalian satire. This is evidenced by his classic work *Gulliver's Travels* in which Swift attacks corrupt politicians and the system which sanctions dishonesty.

Twentieth-century satire

George Bernard Shaw, 'Pygmalion'
One of the great satirists of the twentieth century is the playwright George Bernard Shaw. Shaw was an ardent social reformer and he often used satire as a way of alerting his audience to the injustice within their society in the hope that they might begin to effect some changes.

     Through the character of Eliza Doolittle in *Pygmalion*, Shaw satirises the class system. Eliza is a cockney flower girl, a young woman whose speech reveals her humble social status. The title 'Pygmalion' refers to a Greek sculptor who fell in love with his own statue of Galatea. In Shaw's play, Eliza is the Pygmalion of Henry Higgins, a gentleman and a phonetician who resolves to raise Eliza's social status simply by improving her speech. He does so, but in the process reveals his own arrogance and insensitivity, which is in stark contrast to Eliza's simple good sense and compassion. Social class, Shaw implies, has a lot to do with proper speech; but genuine class has more to do with whether or not people treat each other with respect.

Shaw also satirises, in the figures of Eliza and Higgins, the conventions of romantic comedy. The audience expects Eliza and Higgins will fall in love and marry but this Shaw resolutely avoids. At the end of the play, Eliza has left Higgins to marry the simple but devoted young gentleman Freddy Hill.

Tutorial

Progress questions
1. Explain the difference between a static character and a dynamic character.

2. Explain the difference between a character treated ironically and one treated satirically.

Seminar discussion
1. Why is the dramatic monologue genre particularly appropriate for revealing character?

2. By depicting character ironically, writers often produce satiric results. How is this possible?

3. Is there a limit to how cruel satire should be?

4. What sort of characters do you think people identify with most easily?

Practical assignment
With a group of friends, discuss the term 'stereotype' and decide how each of you would be characterised stereotypically.

Study and revision tip
Make up a list of the main characters who inhabit the literary works you are studying. Beside the names list two or three adjectives which best describe these characters. Do the adjectives suggest that the character is static, dynamic or stereotypical?

8

The Influence of the Narrator

One-minute overview – A story needs a storyteller. The stance from which the storyteller or **narrator** tells the story is known as the **point-of-view**. Sometimes the narrator will be **omniscient**, capable of telling readers the thoughts and actions of all the characters at any time. Sometimes the narrator will limit him or herself to relaying to readers the thoughts and actions of the main character only; such a storyteller is known as a **limited omniscient** narrator. The narrator will sometimes be a character in the story. A **first-person-major-character-narrator** tells a story in which he or she is the protagonist (see Chapter 2). From this point-of-view, the narrator can describe his or her thoughts but can only speculate on the thoughts of other characters. A **first-person-minor-character-narrator** participates in a minor way in the story but primarily observes and describes the actions of the main character and reports those to the readers. From this point-of-view, the narrator can only speculate on the main character's thoughts. An author will try, sometimes, to render the narrator invisible and tell the story almost exclusively through dialogue. Such a story has an **objective point-of-view**. In this chapter we will explore:

▶ the omniscient narrator
▶ the limited omniscient narrator
▶ first-person, major character as narrator
▶ first-person, minor character as narrator
▶ the objective narrator.

The omniscient narrator

Omniscient means all-knowing. An omniscient narrator is like a god who can provide readers with all of the information they could ever want. An omniscient narrator can tell us what all of the characters in the story are thinking and what they are doing at any time, in any place. It is a powerful point-of-view, especially effective in novels which contain many interesting and psychologically complex characters and sweeping action which occurs in a number of locales. Its drawbacks are that the narrator is detached, above the action rather than within it, and so it lacks the sense of realism and immediacy we get from a first-person point-of-view.

Example

D. H. Lawrence, 'The Rocking Horse Winner'
Lawrence's 'The Rocking Horse Winner' is a good example of a story narrated from the omniscient point-of-view. The story delves into the minds of two characters and describes a sequence of somewhat supernatural events.

The story opens describing a beautiful woman who is embittered because she has no luck, she has not married well, and she cannot love her children. The narrator quickly moves into the mind of one of the children, Paul, who is determined to stop the voices in the house which chant, 'there must be more money!' He feels he can win his mother's love if he can solve the money problems which so divert her attention.

Paul discovers he can predict the winner of horse races by riding his rocking horse until the motion produces a trance-like effect which culminates in a supernatural experience, during which the winner is magically revealed to him. With the help of the gardener, Bassett, and later his uncle Oscar, Paul puts money on the races and wins a fortune. But the strain makes him seriously ill. He dies after the strain of discovering the winner of the Derby proves to be too much for him.

The omniscient point-of-view is particularly well-suited to 'The Rocking Horse Winner' because the story is, in many ways, a **fable**. A fable is a story which often features supernatural events and characters, notably talking animals, and which contains a clear moral. The moral of this story is that love is more important, especially for the health of a family, than money.

There is an interesting sub-text to 'The Rocking Horse Winner' as well. Some critics suggest Hester's cold heart reflects sexual unfulfilment and that, on a subconscious and Oedipal level, Paul is trying to satisfy her, the demonic rocking on his horse mirroring sexual activity.

The limited omniscient narrator

If the omniscient narrator is a god, the limited-omniscient narrator is a demi-god who delves into the subconscious of only one character in the story, the protagonist. Many short stories, which tend to focus on a single character, are told from the limited omniscient point-of-view.

Example
James Joyce, 'Eveline'
The narrator of Joyce's story 'Eveline' never leaves the side of the main, the title character. In typical limited-omniscient manner, the narrator traces Eveline's actions and tells us what she is thinking.

Eveline is a young Irish woman whose home life has been oppressive ever since the death of her mother. Her father is abusive and refuses to let her have a life of her own. When she meets a young sailor who offers to take her to Buenos Aires, she is tempted. She makes it as far as the quay, but, just before boarding the ship, she has a change of heart. Her sense of obligation to her family outweighs her desire for a whole new life. And she has been a prisoner for so long, she is suddenly afraid of what might happen to her on the outside world.

Notice, as the story nears its end, how effectively the limited-omniscient narrator communicates Eveline's inner feelings without assuming her character:

> All the seas of the world tumbled about her heart. He was drawing her into them: he would drown her. She gripped both hands at the iron railing.

Eveline's hands, gripping the iron railing, symbolise her imprisonment. As the story ends, she stares at Frank but appears not even to recognise him.

The first-person major-character narrator

The first-person major-character narrator is something of an egotist. This narrator tells a story in which he or she is the main character, the focus of attention. The first-person major-character point-of-view, like its poetic cousin, the dramatic monologue (see Chapter 3), is especially effective for revealing the inner thoughts and the personality of a single main character.

Example
Margaret Atwood, 'Rape Fantasies'
Estelle, the first-person narrator of Margaret Atwood's story 'Rape Fantasies', begins by describing her co-workers, as they respond to a magazine article about rape fantasies, by sharing their own. Estelle is witty and sardonic, and, with a well-chosen phrase or two, she cleverly reveals the essence of her friends' personalities.

As the story continues, however, the humour begins to fade, as Estelle tells us about her own rape fantasies. She has had many, and, in nearly all of them, she ends up befriending her would-be rapist with whom she shares something significant, such as a serious illness. In the process, Estelle reveals her true nature. She is a lonely and rather sad young woman who would like to have a serious relationship, but seems unable, except in her fantasy life, to relate to others in any intimate way. Her mordant wit, so entertaining at times, clouds her judgement of others and perhaps scares them away.

The first-person point-of-view reveals Estelle's personality in a way an omniscient narrator could not. An omniscient narrator would not use Estelle's own unique speech patterns and colloquial writing style, which so suit her personality and give us insight into her character. By becoming Estelle, Atwood paints a particularly vivid picture of a unique and interesting character.

The first-person minor-character narrator

If the first-person major-character narrator is an egotist, the first-person minor-character narrator is a gossip. He or she observes the actions of another person, a friend, usually, and then tells the rest of us all about what that friend did, when, and to whom. Just as we like to tell stories which feature ourselves as the focus, we like to observe others and gossip about them. Stories told from the first-person minor-character point-of-view are interesting and engaging because the narrator openly puts his or her own spin on the personality and actions of the main character.

Example
Doris Lessing, 'Our Friend Judith'
Judith Castlewell is the main character of Doris Lessing's story 'Our Friend Judith', but she is not the narrator. The narrator is an unnamed friend who gets the information which comprises the plot of the story from Judith herself and from another friend, Betty.

Judith is a single woman of forty, a poet, beautiful, independent, not particularly social. Her life is of great interest to Betty and the narrator because it is so different from their own and because Judith is such an interesting person. She lives her life the way she wants to, unencumbered by the usual responsibilities of a nine-to-five-job and a demanding family. She travels to Italy on assignment for the BBC and meets Luigi, an Italian barber with whom she has a relationship. He becomes attached to her as does a pregnant cat, too young to have the three kittens she eventually gives birth to. The cat is unable to provide milk for her kittens and they die, one of them killed by the cat herself, one by Luigi. Unable or not knowing how to deal with so much emotional turmoil, Judith returns home to England, to the great disappointment of Luigi and his sister.

Although Judith is clearly the central character of the story, she could not be its narrator. In spite of her education and intelligence, Judith lacks self-knowledge. She is remote and detached from others, but, as the ending of the story makes clear, she sees herself as a more caring person than she really is. Indeed, it is because she is an intellectual, more comfortable with affairs of the head than the heart, that she cannot fathom the interest others take in her. She could not be bothered to tell a story of which she was the centre. Her friends are fascinated by Judith's personality and actions, always trying but never quite succeeding in understanding them. For this reason, the first-person minor-character works well for Lessing's story.

The objective narrator

Sometimes a writer will try to make his or her narrator disappear entirely and rely almost exclusively on dialogue among characters to tell the story. The objective narrator establishes setting in a precise but rather detached style, and then lets the conversation tell the story.

Example
Ernest Hemingway, 'Hills Like White Elephants'
Hemingway's story 'Hills Like White Elephants' is a good example of the use of the objective point-of-view. The story is set in a train station in Spain, which Hemingway describes in a single terse paragraph. Thereafter, a conversation ensues between a young man and a young woman. Occasionally, the dialogue is interrupted by description which, suitably, reads more like stage directions than the voice of a narrator.

The objective point-of-view does seem to turn a story into a play. Dialogue carries the story in which the young man tries to talk the woman into having an abortion so that they might maintain the same carefree lifestyle they have been enjoying for some time. The conversation is intense – the woman resists her lover's persuasive appeal, then she seems to relent, but her final decision remains deliberately ambiguous.

For stories like 'Hills Like White Elephants', in which two characters vie to establish their positions within an intimate relationship, the objective point-of-view is very effective.

Tutorial

Progress questions
1. What is the difference between an omniscient and limited-omniscient point-of-view?

2. Why would an author choose to write a story from the first-person major-character point-of-view?

3. Why would an author choose to write a story from the first-person minor-character point-of-view?

Seminar discussion

1. The works used in this chapter to illustrate point-of-view were all stories. Would point-of-view have the same effect on our interpretation of a narrative poem as it does on our interpretation of a story?

2. Why is point-of-view of little or no importance in drama?

3. What are the advantages of an objective point-of-view?

Practical assignment

Write a first-person account of a recent significant event in your life. Consider how this story would change if a close friend or relative wrote it instead of you.

Study and revision tip

Determine the point-of-view of each of the stories and novels on your reading list, and consider how the narrator influences the plot and the theme and shapes your opinion of the main character.

9

The Influence of Setting

One-minute overview – Compared to character (Chapter 7) and point-of-view (Chapter 8), setting is a straightforward literary element. It simply establishes the **time when** and the **place where** the action of a story, play or poem occurs. Yet setting can have as important an influence on the meaning of a literary work as any other literary element. Setting can be as important to plot (Chapter 6) as character. It can serve a symbolic (Chapter 13) function and resonate with connotations beyond its time and place. Setting can also contribute to the irony of a story. In this chapter we will explore:

▶ setting and plot
▶ setting and symbolism
▶ setting and irony
▶ setting and metaphor.

Setting and plot

The community in which we live can influence our personalities and our actions. People who are from small towns think people from big cities are harried and rather rude; people from major cities think small-towners are slow and rather simple. Similarly, citizens of one country tend to have different values and attitudes from citizens of another, and when we travel to another place, our behaviour is usually mediated by local history, culture and custom. In other words, the time and place (the setting) where the action (the plot) occurs influences human events and behaviour.

Example
William Trevor, 'Beyond the Pale'
William Trevor's story 'Beyond the Pale' is set in Ireland but its

main characters are English. When an author places English people in an Irish setting, the setting is likely to influence the plot because of the historical relationship between those two countries. The story is about four bridge partners who holiday together each year at an idyllic Irish country inn. To these four comfortably-off English people, Ireland is a utopia, and 'the Troubles' do not exist. The relationships between the bridge partners are complex. Strafe is married to Cynthia but has an open affair with Dorothy, the first-person minor-character (see Chapter 8) narrator of the story. Strafe leaves the room he shares with his wife and visits Dorothy in her room on a regular basis. Cynthia is supposed to turn a blind eye to her husband's infidelity, as all of them turn a blind eye to the Irish-Catholic struggle for independence and the social consequences of that struggle. But, on this visit, politics enters paradise when another hotel guest befriends Cynthia, and tells her about his childhood sweetheart who moved to London to plant bombs for the IRA. A bomb she was building exploded and killed her. Later, overwrought by the tragedy, the guest wanders into the ocean and drowns himself.

At first, Cynthia is devastated by the experience, but, as she recovers, she confronts the truth. Her first truth is the responsibility she and her compatriots share for the civil war in Ireland and for the agony it has caused. Cynthia becomes conscious of her setting not as an idyllic holiday resort but as a real place with social problems she and her bridge partners, representatives of the English middle class, have ignored for too long. Her second truth is that, by ignoring her husband's infidelity with a supposed friend, she has lost her own self-respect. She recovers it in the course of an intensely dramatic confrontation scene at the end of the story.

In 'Beyond the Pale', the setting incites the development of the political dimension of the plot which, in turn, results in Cynthia's personal liberation. The narrator, Dorothy, refuses to acknowledge either Irish politics or the significance of Cynthia's outburst, which she regards as the ravings of a mad woman.

The English, Trevor seems to be saying, are making progress, but there are many still who believe the problem will go away if they ignore it. Cynthia proves the English can overcome their indifference to their relationship with Ireland; but Dorothy believes the solution is to blame the victim.

Setting and symbolism

In some works of literature, the setting is more than the time and the place. It suggests a condition or a desire which transcends the where and the when of the action; in other words, the setting can serve a symbolic function.

Example
Robert Frost, 'Stopping By Woods On A Snowy Evening'
The setting of Frost's much-anthologised poem, 'Stopping By Woods On A Snowy Evening', is clearly established by its title. The narrator of the poem stops to appreciate the beauty of a winter night in the New England woods, comments on how he would like to remain, then, realising he has 'promises to keep/And miles to go before I sleep' (lines 15–16), continues on his journey.

Some literary critics feel the dark woods symbolise death, and that the poem's narrator is, in fact, contemplating suicide. He feels guilty about stopping, his horse is agitated, it is 'the darkest evening of the year' (line 8), and the woods are 'dark and deep' (line 13). Moreover, the repetition of the last line implies a 'sleep' beyond a single night. In the end, the narrator rejects death, symbolised by the macabre appeal the dark woods have for him, knowing that too many people depend upon him. The poem's symbolism is conveyed by its haunting setting.

Setting and irony

The setting adds to the irony of a literary work when there is a disconnection between that setting and the events taking place within it. It is ironic when a murder occurs in a church or when a war breaks out on Christmas Day.

Example
Henry Reed, 'Naming of Parts'
Henry Reed's poem, 'The Naming of Parts', is set in spring time

amidst japonica glistening 'like coral' (line 5), silent almond blossoms and fragrant flowers. It is a setting perfect for romance or peaceful contemplation. Instead, the Royal Army Ordnance Corps (in which Reed served) is in training to fight in the Second World War and is learning the names of the parts of their rifles under the command of a stern and humourless sergeant major.

In this juxtaposition between an Eden-like setting and a lesson on the naming of the parts of a rifle, Reed conveys the anti-war theme, typical of much of his poetry.

Setting and metaphor

A metaphor (discussed in detail in Chapter 11) is a comparison, the purpose of which is to clarify or intensify the more complex of the objects of the comparison. By saying, as Plutarch does, that 'poetry is painting that speaks', we understand more clearly what Plutarch means and how he feels about poetry.

Example
William Shakespeare, 'Full Many a Glorious Morning Have I Seen'
In his 33rd sonnet, Shakespeare compares the literal sun to the sunshine of his own life, his great friend, who inspired his sonnet sequence. The sun in the sky shines brightly, the poet says, but can be eclipsed by a single cloud. Similarly, the poet's friend can shine the light of his friendship on the poet, but then turn his attention to someone else. We would expect the poet to be crushed by his friend's fickleness, but the poet takes his metaphor to its more logical conclusion. If the sun in the heavens can be blotted out, he says, I can hardly expect my earthly sun to shine only for me:

> Yet him for this my love no whit disdaineth:
> Suns of the world may stain when heaven's sun staineth.
>   (lines 13–14)

The sonnet's setting, then, is used as a metaphor for a friend's devotion.

Tutorial

Progress questions

1. Define the term 'irony'. Describe how the setting of a literary work could be ironic.

2. Define the term 'metaphor'. Describe how the setting of a literary work could be used metaphorically to intensify or clarify a poem, story or play.

3. Provide an example of a symbolic use of setting in a poem, a story or a play not discussed in this book.

Seminar discussion

1. Consider the influence of setting on gender.

   (a) In what literary settings are men more privileged than women?

   (b) In what settings are women more privileged than men?

2. Compare and contrast the setting of a typical science fiction story with the setting of a typical romantic comedy.

Practical assignment

Think about the setting, the time and the place, in which you now live. Consider how your own setting has shaped your personality, values and ideals.

Study and revision tip

Note the settings of each literary work you are or will be studying and consider the ways in which the setting influences other elements in those poems, stories and plays.

10

Getting the Message

One-minute overview – Answer these three questions: What things in life are most important to you? What are the most significant social issues of our time? What stages do most people pass through in the course of a lifetime? Your answers – family, faith, work, friends, intimate relationships, education; war, poverty, ecology; childhood, adolescence, marriage, parenthood, old age, death – identify the common topics of literature. Most poems, stories and plays come with a message, often more than one, about an important issue. Authors usually try to enlighten their readers as well as entertain them. Writers relate the complete variety of human experience and try, in the process, to give their readers some insight into the significance of that experience. The literary term for the message, the insight into human experience an author offers to his or her readers, is **theme**. In this chapter, we will explore seven of the most common literary themes, illustrated with reference to a widely taught poem or story. The themes are:

▶ family
▶ love
▶ war
▶ nature
▶ death
▶ faith
▶ time.

Family

Since family is our basic social unit, it stands to reason that writers will often tell of the love and conflict, the function and the dysfunction, inevitably found within any family.

Example

Katherine Mansfield, 'The Daughters of the Late Colonel'

In this story, Katherine Mansfield describes the relationship between a father and his two daughters. The girls fear their father, a retired army colonel, who has totally dominated their lives. His death will change their lives, though they are not certain exactly how. They have completely lost their ability to assert themselves. The father's nurse exploits their kindness, and their maid is insolent and indifferent to their needs. As the story ends, they hear a noisy organ grinder and their immediate response is to rush outside and give the organ grinder money so he will move on quickly and not disturb their father. They realise suddenly they don't have to live their lives catering to their father's every need and whim as they had to in the past. Clearly the sudden freedom has confused them, and it might even be too late for them to adjust to the new life their father's death offers.

A theme of the 'The Daughters of the Late Colonel' is that parents wield considerable power in shaping their children's personalities, and that parents who are too authoritarian can mould children into adults unable to stand up for themselves.

Love

Love is another common literary theme. Most writers, poets especially, have paid tribute in verse to the man or woman they love.

Example

Elizabeth Barrett Browning, 'How Do I Love Thee'

One of the most famous of such tributes is Elizabeth Barrett Browning's sonnet, 'How Do I Love Thee', written to express her love for her husband, Robert. Her poem expresses a common sentiment in poems of this nature: our love is not merely physical; it is righteous and spiritual as well:

> I love thee freely, as men strive for Right;
> I love thee purely, as they turn from Praise.
>   (lines 7–8)

Barrett Browning's theme is that true love is a spiritual union of two souls, a union which will last unto eternity.

War

War is another common subject for works of literature. There are poems and stories which celebrate the courage and honour displayed in a time of war, but by and large poets and story-tellers write of the horrors of war, the tragic and futile loss of human life and property.

Example
Wilfred Owen, 'Futility'
Owen is perhaps the best-known poet of the First World War (1914–18) in the English language. In his heart-breaking sonnet, 'Futility', he writes of a young soldier, killed on the battlefields of France.

'Move him into the sun', the poem begins, as the speaker makes a futile and desperate attempt to bring the boy back to life as the sun woke him from sleep back home. The sun has enormous power, awakening seeds and even 'Woke once the clays of a cold star' (line 9). But the sun meets its match on the killing fields of France and can never bring the young soldier back to life.

Owen's theme is that the greatest of war's many evils is its inevitable waste of young life.

Nature

Authors, poets especially, often celebrate the beauty of nature and describe the soothing effect nature's beauty has on them.

Example
John Keats, 'To Autumn'
In his ode 'To Autumn', Keats describes the sense of tranquillity nature gives us when, in the autumn, she is at her richest and most radiant.

1. In the first stanza, he describes, with vivid imagery, the ripe fruit, the plump gourds and hazel shells, and the late autumn flowers, still radiantly blooming.

2. In the second stanza, he writes of the harvest, and personifies autumn as a beautiful farm worker, 'Thy hair soft-lifted by the winnowing wind' (line 15), as she reaps the harvest, rests, and watches 'the last oozings' of the cyder-press.

3. In the third and final stanza, Keats describes the music of autumn, the gnats mourning the end of summer, the lambs bleating, the soft treble of the red-breast's whistle.

Keats' theme is that when there is perfect harmony within the natural world there can, as well, be perfect harmony within the human world.

Death

The bumper sticker reads 'Life is hard and then you die'. But as a literary theme, death is rarely an occasion for exasperation and sorrow but more often an opportunity for speculation about the immortality of the human soul.

Example
William Butler Yeats, 'Sailing to Byzantium' and 'Byzantium'
In 'Sailing to Byzantium', Yeats writes about his own desire for immortality. He loved Byzantine art and architecture and yearns to be reincarnated as a Byzantine *objet d'art*, specifically a bird carved in gold. He will leave Ireland to the young, he says, and, after his death, his soul will 'sail' to Byzantium. There he will continue his role as a poet, prophet and historian, of Byzantium now, not Ireland.

In a later, related poem, 'Byzantium', Yeats imagines he has achieved his goal. His soul has sailed to Byzantium, and now, as the golden bird, 'In glory of changeless metal' (line 22), watches other souls arrive, go through the purification ritual, and achieve immortality.

Yeats' theme is that death may be the end of physical life, but it is also an opportunity for spiritual reincarnation.

Faith

The loss and/or the recovery of faith has long been a common literary theme.

Example
John Donne, 'Batter My Heart, Three-Personed God'
An Anglican priest, Donne occasionally expressed doubts in his poetry about the strength of his commitment to his God. In his sonnet, 'Batter My Heart', he writes of the pull of temptation and fears he is drifting away from God's authority. In the poem, he asks God to batter his heart, to break him and burn him because to be broken by the love of God is to be made whole again. He asks God to imprison him because to be imprisoned by God's love is to be set free; he asks God to ravish him because to be ravished by God's love is to be rendered chaste.

Donne's sonnet is built around a series of **paradoxes**. A **paradox** is a phrase which seems self-contradictory but, in fact, makes powerful sense by virtue of its lack of logic. When Donne asks God to 'overthrow' him so that he might 'rise and stand', he seems to be making no sense. But his theme is that we can only rise and stand when God's love knocks us down, and his use of paradox is an effective way of reinforcing this theme.

Time

Writers are often struck by the transience of time and the brevity of human life. Often in their work, they urge us to make the most of the time available to us. The **carpe diem** or 'seize the day' theme is a common one. The writer reminds readers that time flies and that life must be lived to the full.

Example
A. E. Housman, 'Loveliest of Trees'
In 'Loveliest of Trees', Houseman describes a beautiful spring

scene, the focus of which is a cherry tree 'hung with bloom' (line 2). He is twenty years old and reasons that he has only fifty more springs to appreciate nature's beauty. Since 'Fifty springs are little room' (line 10) to admire nature's beauty, he resolves to return to this place in the winter 'To see the cherry hung with snow' (line 12). Life is brief, Housman says, and we must appreciate nature's beauty, regardless of the season.

Tutorial

Progress questions

1. How can a character in a play, story or narrative poem 'carry' the theme of the work? Provide an example or two.

2. How might the point-of-view chosen by an author to narrate a literary work influence the theme of that work? Provide two examples.

Seminar discussion

1. Love is a common literary theme. What other dimensions of relationships between men and women do writers explore in their work?

2. The beauty of nature is a common literary theme. What qualities of the natural world, besides its beauty, do writers describe?

3. What would you identify as the top ten list of most common themes based on your own reading?

Practical assignment

Literary themes can often be expressed as famous old adages, for example:

Time flies.
Love is blind.
A rolling stone gathers no moss.

List five such adages and a literary work which reflects each one.

Study and revision tip

Review the poems, stories and plays on your reading list and try to express the theme of each one in a single sentence.

11

The Effect of Metaphor

One-minute overview – A **metaphor** is a comparison, the purpose of which is to clarify or intensify the more complex of the objects of the comparison. For example, we might say that a person is 'a real peach' or 'a rock' or 'a flower child' or 'a pain in the neck' or 'a space cadet' or a 'sweetheart'. We are using metaphor to help convey that person's personality or behaviour. A **simile** is a type of metaphor which makes the comparison explicit by using either the word 'like' or the word 'as'. Marlene Dietrich used a simile when she sang, in *The Blue Angel*, 'men cluster to me <u>like</u> moths around a flame'. Another form of metaphor is **personification** which compares something non-human with something that is. When Ralph Hodgson wrote 'Time you old gypsy man,/Will you not stay?' he was personifying time as a gypsy, always moving on. A **hyperbole** is a metaphor which bases its comparison on the use of exaggeration. When Al Jolson said of his mother 'I'd walk a million miles for one of your smiles', he was using hyperbole to indicate the depth of his affection. **Litotes** is a deliberate use of understatement, usually to create an ironic or satiric effect. When a teacher criticises her students for not grasping a simple point by saying 'this is not rocket science', she is using litotes. **Metonymy** is a specific form of metaphor in which a phrase is understood to represent something more. When the press says the Prime Minister is 'sabre rattling', readers understand the use of the metaphor for 'threatening war'. Similarly, a **synecdoche** is the use of a part to represent a whole, as in the expression 'lend me a hand'. In literature, a metaphor can develop character, clarify theme and intensify symbolism. In this chapter we will explore:

▶ metaphor and character
▶ metaphor and theme
▶ metaphor and symbolism.

Metaphor and character

A metaphor is a comparison, the purpose of which is to clarify or intensify the more complex of the objects of the comparison. A metaphor can help develop a character and clarify a character's actions and motivation.

Example

Stevie Smith, 'Not Waving but Drowning'

A wave of the hand is an interesting metaphor. It can represent, among other things, a friendly greeting or a plea for help.

Stevie Smith uses this metaphor in her poem 'Not Waving but Drowning' to make a comment on our indifference to the suffering of our fellow humanity. The narrator is swimming in the ocean and his waves are mistaken for friendly waves, when they are, in fact, pleas for help from a drowning man. The cold water of the ocean becomes a metaphor for life. 'I was much too far out all my life' (line 11), the narrator says, referring more to his emotional state than his ocean swim. The narrator needs emotional support but those who see his wave prefer to interpret it as a casual sign of friendship, rather than a cry for help. A cry for help would require the effort of emotional support we prefer to withhold.

Metaphor and theme

In addition to helping establish character, a metaphor can be used to intensify the theme of a literary work.

Example

John Donne, 'A Valediction: Forbidding Mourning'

In this poem, Donne uses a striking metaphor to intensify his theme. He compares the love he has for his wife with the love other couples share, and pronounces the love he shares with his wife superior because it is spiritual as much as physical.

The poet is leaving the country on business and urges his wife not to mourn his absence. Because of their spiritual bond, he says, wherever he goes, he takes her with him. He compares the two of them to the two feet of a mathematical compass. Her soul is 'the

fixt foot' (line 26) and 'leanes, and hearkens after' the other foot
when it goes away. Together, they form a circle, a symbol of both
perfection and a wedding band. They come together again when
the wandering foot returns:

> Thy firmnes drawes my circle just,
> And makes me end, where I begunne.
> (lines 35–36)

Ingenious, elaborate metaphors such as the one Donne uses in 'A
Valediction: Forbidding Mourning' are called **conceits**.

Metaphor and symbolism

A metaphor is a comparison between two objects. Sometimes a
writer will augment the comparison by ascribing symbolic
connotations to one of the objects which comprise the comparison.

Example
Emily Dickinson, 'There's a Certain Slant of Light'
In her complex poem, Emily Dickinson identifies the 'slant of
light' on a winter afternoon as 'the Seal Despair'. The metaphor is
intriguing. Despair is unpleasant but transitory, and when we
recover from despair, we feel renewed.

> When it goes, 'tis like the Distance
> On the look of Death.
> (lines 15–16)

Some critics feel the 'slant of light' has additional symbolic
connotations because of the poem's religious context. The light
'oppresses, like the Heft/Of Cathedral Tunes' (lines 3–4). It gives
us a 'heavenly Hurt' (line 5). Some readers feel the slant of light
symbolises the immortality of the soul. Death brings despair but
the soul's immortality transcends that despair. The series of
paradoxes around which the poem is built – the heft of cathedral
tunes, heavenly hurt, the seal despair, an imperial affliction –
convey the sorrow of death countermanded by the triumph of the
human soul.

Tutorial

Progress questions

1. What is the difference between a simile and a metaphor?

2. What is personification?

3. What is the difference between metaphor and symbolism?

Seminar discussion

1. How can a writer use metaphor to help develop a character? Provide two or three examples.

2. How can a writer use metaphor to intensify theme? Provide two or three examples.

3. Can a metaphor be a symbol?

Practical assignment

Invent some creative metaphors or similes which effectively describe your parents, siblings and several of your friends.

Study and revision tip

Consider the use of metaphor in five poems on your reading list. Think about how the metaphors help you to understand and appreciate those poems.

12

The Effect of Imagery

One-minute overview – In literature, an image is a word picture: a phrase, a sentence or a line. It enhances readers' appreciation of the figurative more than the literal meaning of a poem, story or play. In other words, writers use imagery to help their readers get a better *sense* of what the writer is trying to communicate. We use the word 'sense' instead of 'understanding' because an image is sensual: it arouses in readers one or more of the five senses. Through the use of an effective image, a writer can help us see or hear or taste or touch or smell what it is he or she is describing. When the narrator of Diane Ackerman's poem 'Beija Flor' says that when her lover kisses her, 'sunset pours molasses down my spine/and, in my hips, the green wings of the jungle flutter' (lines 13–14), she uses vivid images to help convey the sensual pleasure she is experiencing. Imagery can advance the plot of a story, define character, animate setting and clarify theme. In this chapter we will explore:

▶ imagery and plot
▶ imagery and character
▶ imagery and setting
▶ imagery and theme.

Imagery and plot

Imagery is associated with the artistry of a literary work; plot more with its structure and literal meaning. Yet imagery can signal the direction a plot will take.

Example
Ambrose Bierce, 'An Occurrence at Owl Creek Bridge'
The plot of Ambrose Bierce's American Civil War story concerns a Confederate Southern farmer, Peyton Farquar, who is about to be

hanged for blowing up a bridge of strategic importance to the enemy. The rope, suspended from the side of Owl Creek Bridge, snaps with Farquar's weight, and he escapes. He makes his way on to shore, dodging Federal bullets, struggles through the woods, and eventually makes his way back home. But when he is about to embrace his wife, he feels a jolt to his neck. The story ends with a stark description of Farquar hanging from the Owl Creek Bridge. His escape had been a deathbed fantasy.

It is the imagery Bierce uses that first alerts us to the unreality of Farquar's experience. Bierce describes a man whose senses have been honed to supernatural levels. As Farquar emerges from the water and enters the forest, he can see 'the brilliant-bodied flies, the gray spiders stretching their webs from twig to twig.' He notes 'the prismatic colors in all the dewdrops upon a million blades of grass.' He hears the 'audible music' of the 'humming of the gnats that danced above the eddies of the stream, the beating of the dragon-flies' wings, the strokes of the water-spiders' legs.' Throughout Farquar's escape fantasy, Bierce uses similar vivid imagery to reflect the perceptions of a man whose senses have been heightened to supernatural levels as he experiences the moment of his own death.

Readers realise, in retrospect, that this imagery signalled the direction the plot was taking. Farquar's escape could not be real because his powers of perception, reflected in Bierce's striking images, were far too acute to be normal. In fact, those images suggested the sharpened sense of sight and sound Bierce imagines a man might experience at the moment of his death.

Imagery and character

Imagery can also be used to help readers visualise a character whom a writer is describing.

Example

Lord Byron, 'She Walks in Beauty'
Byron's famous poem is a good example of the use of imagery to describe physical appearance. The poem describes the beautiful wife of Byron's cousin. Byron first met her in June of 1814, and

wrote the poem almost immediately thereafter. She was in mourning and wore a black dress, covered in spangles.

The imagery Byron uses helps his readers see a striking dark woman in a black, glowing dress. She is like the night 'of cloudless climes, and starry skies' (line 2). Her hair 'waves in every raven tress' then 'lightens o'er her face' (lines 9–10). The innocent face framed by the raven hair parallels the mellow light the stars emit, amid the black night. The imagery in the first two stanzas prepare readers for the impression conveyed in the final stanza of the woman's winning smile, eloquent demeanour and gentle heart.

Imagery and setting

Imagery is a very important literary device for establishing setting. Writers want their readers to be able to visualise the place where the action of their poem or story takes place, to hear its sounds and absorb its ambience. Through the effective use of imagery, writers can help give readers a sense of place.

Example
Dylan Thomas, 'Fern Hill'
Fern Hill was the name of the Welsh farmhouse where the poet Dylan Thomas spent his boyhood summers. Thomas immortalises the farm in this poem. His use of imagery creates an indelible picture in the reader's mind of a boy in tune with nature, as he enjoys the freedom of his summer holidays. At his command, Thomas writes, the trees on the farm 'Trail with daisies and barley/Down the rivers of the windfall light' (lines 8–9). The 'foxes on the hills barked clear and cold' (line 16). The sun seemed to set the grass on fire. Fern Hill is utopia, quite literally, as Thomas makes clear in the fourth stanza of this six-stanza poem, the 'Garden of Eden'.

Thomas writes the poem from the perspective of an adult who knows he cannot turn back the hands of time and relive his past. He knows now time held him 'green and dying' (line 53) even during those carefree days on Fern Hill. But the focus of the poem is on the boy's sense of community with all *living* things, as the poem's imagery makes clear.

Indeed, 'Fern Hill' is a feast of imagery. In the word picture Thomas paints, readers see the young boy at play on his farm, hear the songs of the owls and the night-jars, and sense the pastoral innocence of the poem's setting.

Imagery and theme

Imagery can be used to underscore the theme of a poem. Indeed, between 1912 and 1917, there was a group of poets who called themselves **imagists**, and their aim was to write poetry which accented imagery or, their preferred term, **imagism**, to communicate the poem's meaning.

The haiku

The imagists were influenced by the Japanese **haiku**, a brief poem, consisting of a single image. A Japanese haiku consists of three lines of five, seven and five syllables, respectively:

> Fir trees hang pine cones.
> Winter winds freeze autumn leaves.
> Pine cones in warm snow.

English haiku writers tend to deviate from this rigid structure while still producing a single-image poem.

Example

Ezra Pound, 'In a Station of the Metro'
Ezra Pound was a leading exponent of the imagist school. His haiku, 'In a Station of the Metro', consists of fourteen words:

> The apparition of these faces in the crowd,
> Petals on a wet, black bough.

The poem is a single image of faces in a crowded metro station. The faces are compared to petals which have dropped onto the black bough of a tree after rain. This connection between the human world and the natural world is typical of the haiku genre. This theme – that human and natural worlds are inextricably connected – is established through the single image Pound presents.

Tutorial

Progress questions
1. How might imagery influence the plot of a literary work? Provide two examples.

2. How can imagery help to define character? Provide two examples.

3. Why is imagery important in establishing setting?

Seminar discussion
1. A literary theme appeals to our reason; imagery to our senses. What is the nature of the relationship between imagery and theme?

2. Metaphors are often important components of an image. Why is this?

Practical assignment
Try writing a haiku yourself. Start by thinking of an idea, and some images to use to express it.

Study and revision tip
Consider the influence of imagery on the plots, characters, themes and settings of the literary works on your reading list.

13

Analysing Symbols

One-minute overview – A symbol is an element within a literary work, an element with more than a literal meaning. In fact, some symbols, known as **universal** or **cultural** symbols, do not require the context of literature to communicate their non-literal meaning. For example, we wave our country's flag at an international sporting event and all recognise the flag as a symbol of support and national pride. If we send a dozen long-stem red roses to someone, the recipient understands the roses as a symbol of our affection. A **contextual** symbol is one which has non-literal meaning only within the context of the work of art in which it is found. The farmer in Breughel's painting 'Landscape With the Fall of Icarus' is a contextual symbol of human indifference; Icarus himself (who tried to fly to the sun but fell to his death when his wax wings melted) is a universal symbol of the energy of the human spirit. Anything – any object or element of nature – within a work of literature can have symbolic overtones. Even a character in a work of literature might represent or symbolise something which transcends the character's literal role or function in the story. In this chapter we will explore:

▶ objects as symbols
▶ natural symbols
▶ religious symbols
▶ character as symbol.

Objects as symbols

Any object in a work of literature can have symbolic overtones:

1. A handgun might be a phallic symbol.

2. A coffee spoon might symbolise dull routine.
3. A broken clock might symbolise death.

Example

John Keats, 'Ode on a Grecian Urn'
The Grecian urn in Keats' famous ode is a symbol of the harmony of
life, of the integral relationship between the real and the imagined.
The poet studies the paintings on a Grecian urn and is struck by the
realisation that art freezes time. The young woman and the young
man who is pursuing her will never grow old and die: 'For ever wilt
thou love,' he says to the young man, 'and she be fair!' (line 20).

But when he sees another painting on the urn, depicting
sacrifice and death, the poet realises that even a work of art
reminds us of the impermanence of life. Art is beautiful, but it is
also true. The urn 'dost tease us out of thought' (line 44) by
promising a pastoral and eternal world which does not really exist.
But, in the end, the urn is 'a friend to man' (line 48) because it
reminds us that beauty reflects truth and in truth there is beauty.
The symbolism of the Grecian urn is established in the poem's
famous last lines:

'Beauty is truth, truth beauty,' – that is all
    Ye know on earth, and all ye need to know.
        (lines 49–50)

Natural symbols

Writers frequently use as symbols elements within the natural
world:

(a) Blake's tiger (see Chapter 3), for example, symbolises nature's
    power and energy.

(b) Coleridge's albatross in 'The Rime of the Ancient Mariner' (see
    Chapter 3) symbolises the sanctity of nature against which
    humanity must not sin.

(c) The lake, in Maxine Kumin's poem 'Morning Swim', is a symbol of the intimate physical link between the human and natural worlds.

Example

Emily Dickinson, 'I Heard A Fly Buzz'

Emily Dickinson uses a fly as a symbol in her poem 'I Heard A Fly Buzz'. At the moment of her death, the narrator of the poem hears a fly buzz. The occasion is solemn. The narrator has made her will, 'Signed away/What portion of me be/Assignable' (lines 9–11). Now she is dying and her family has gathered beside her bed. As her death comes, 'There interposed a Fly – '(line 12); she hears the fly buzz:

> And then the Windows failed – and then
> I could not see to see –
>   (lines 15–16)

The fly is symbolic, though readers cannot agree on what the fly symbolises. Some readers feel it represents Satan, because we associate flies with filth and germs, and therefore suggests the speaker has not made it to heaven. Other readers feel the fly symbolises the insignificance of death because it is such a common household pest. Its presence in the room undercuts the solemnity of the occasion while it reminds us that death is an everyday occurrence. Still other readers feel the fly symbolises the immortality of the soul, buzzing on even after the body has died.

Dickinson's poem illustrates the versatility of symbolism. A symbol can push a literary work in several different directions at once. The reader decides the direction in which symbolism pushes meaning.

Religious symbols

Religious symbolism is used widely in literature. Usually, a religious symbol will be used to suggest the need for faith or a crisis of faith a main character is suffering.

Example

James Joyce, 'Araby'

In Joyce's story 'Araby', a young adolescent boy experiences his first case of puppy love. The object of his affection is the older sister of his friend, Mangan. He stalks her, and finally works up the courage to speak to her, promising to bring her a present from the fair (called 'Araby') which he will be attending. But he arrives at the fair late, and he overhears a shop girl flirting inanely with two young men. The experience destroys his idealist view of love, and crushes the illusion of his love for Mangan's sister.

'Araby' is a typical 'loss of innocence' story. The boy, who is the first-person narrator (see Chapter 8) of the story, learns that Arabian night fantasies of flawless women perched upon pedestals exist in romance novels but not in real life.

On a symbolic level, the boy learns something else, as well. He learns that in his native Ireland, the Church is a shell of its former self. Throughout the story, the author makes reference to many religious objects and traditions. In the first paragraph of the story, Joyce describes a central apple tree and a rusty bicycle pump in the boy's yard, symbolising a corrupt Garden of Eden and the loss of innocence the boy will experience. The former tenant of the house was a priest, and the house still contains some of the priest's religious books. The boy imagines that he bears a chalice, the cup that holds the communion wine, 'safely through a throng of foes'. Mangan's sister turns a bracelet made of silver, a symbol of Judas's betrayal of Christ, around her wrist while she talks to the boy. When the boy finally arrives at Araby, he recognises 'a silence like that which pervades a church after a service.' He hears the sound of falling coins, reminiscent of the biblical story of the money changers in the temple.

'Araby' is, on the surface, the story of a young boy's unfulfilled quest for romantic love. Symbolically, it is a story of his unfulfilled quest for a true faith. His quest is unfulfilled because the Church has been corrupted by material concerns, and has, in fact, betrayed its flock. The chalice, symbolically the Holy Grail, has not been found. The Church is literally silent; the story's symbolism suggest a spiritual silence, as well.

Character as symbol

A character in a literary work occasionally does double duty. A character can be both a participant in the action, and a symbol which transcends action and suggests deeper meaning. Archetypal or stereotypical characters, discussed in Chapter 7, are examples of one type of symbolic characters.

Example

Nathaniel Hawthorne, 'Young Goodman Brown'
Goodman Brown, the main character in Hawthorne's classic story, is both a character and a symbol. He is a young man, recently married, on his way to a Black Mass. He is ashamed of the evil thoughts that draw him towards the devil but stunned to meet so many people he knows from his village of Salem, who are also on their way to participate in the Mass. In fact, they are all looking forward to the initiation of the latest converts.

Several times throughout the story, Brown hesitates, but the forces of darkness are too much for him. Eventually, he learns that he will not be the only new convert on this night, that a young woman will also be initiated into the ways of evil. When the woman turns out to be his wife, ironically named Faith, he knows he is lost. But just as Faith is about to commit herself to Satan, a puff of smoke clouds the forest and Goodman Brown finds himself back home in Salem. Readers are left to wonder if the experience was real or if it was a dream. Whatever the case, Brown is a changed man from that time forward. He becomes a bitter man, an eternal pessimist, who can never find happiness.

Goodman Brown is a character in a story, but also a symbol of a certain psychological frame of mind. Brown is tempted by sin and ashamed of his weakness. To atone for his guilt he decides, subconsciously, that if *he* is tempted, everyone else must be as well. If everyone is tempted by sin, no one can be good. If no one is good, how is it possible to have faith, hope and charity? Brown is the stereotypical pessimist who goes through life, perpetually gloomy and embittered because he has to believe, as the devil tells him, that 'evil is the nature of mankind'.

Allegory

The symbolism of Brown's character turns 'Young Goodman Brown' into something of an **allegory.** An allegory is a story in which the characters and events extend beyond the confines of their story to represent an object lesson to readers. Characters' names often telegraph the nature of the lesson.

In John Bunyan's *The Pilgrim's Progress*, for example, the main character is Christian who is told by Evangelist to seek the Celestial City. On his way, he encounters such people as Faithful, Hopeful and Giant Despair. The object lesson in *The Pilgrim's Progress* is that personal salvation is available only through a commitment to Christ. Similarly, in 'Young Goodman Brown' there is a character named Faith whom Goodman Brown doubts and ultimately turns away from. The object lesson in this story is that if you don't look for the good in people, you are likely to lose your faith in your own humanity.

Tutorial

Progress questions

1. In your own words, define the term symbolism as it relates to literature.

2. What is a phallic symbol and why are phallic symbols common in literary works?

3. Why are religious symbols often found in literary works?

4. What is the difference between a symbol and a metaphor?

Seminar discussion

1. How can a work of literature be enriched when a character is also a symbol? How can it be diminished when a character is also a symbol?

2. Can anything be a symbol?

3. Who determines whether or not an element in a literary work is a symbol, the reader or the writer?

Practical assignment

Write a paragraph in which you explain the difference between a universal and a contextual symbol. Provide an example of each.

Study and revision tip

While you read the literary works on your reading list, underline those objects, natural elements, religious elements and characters which might have symbolic overtones. When you re-read those works, note in the margin of your text what those elements might symbolise.

14

Listening to the Tone

One-minute overview – Tone refers to the attitude or personality which a literary work projects. The tone can be very serious and solemn, as it is in Milton's *Paradise Lost* (see Chapter 3) or light-hearted and amusing, as it is in 'The Ruined Maid' (see Chapter 6). Tone is the product of the subject of a literary work and the way in which the writer uses language – imagery, metaphor, diction – to describe the subject. In poetry, the rhythm and meter of the lines can also influence the tone. The subject of Elizabeth Barrett Browning's sonnet 'How Do I Love Thee' (see Chapter 10) is the spiritual nature of her love for her husband. She uses expansive imagery, religious metaphors, repetition and slow moving iambic lines to establish the poem's serene and confident tone. Tone can range from the solemn to the light-hearted. Falling somewhere in between these two extremes are some more common literary tones. In this chapter we will explore:

▶ sorrow
▶ resignation
▶ irony
▶ triumph.

Sorrow

When a writer deals with a sad subject, the tone of his or her poem or story will reflect that sorrow.

Example
William Butler Yeats, 'When You Are Old'
The subject of Yeats' poem, 'When You Are Old', is the death of love. The poet addresses a woman he loved, inviting her, when she is old and grey, to read his work and remember the love he had for

her. It was a special, a spiritual love; he was the one man to love the 'pilgrim soul' (line 7) in her. She will be sad to realise that love has gone and remember wistfully the promise of their youth.

The tone of 'When You Are Old' perfectly complements its subject. The dominant image of an old woman falling asleep beside the fire and reading a book of the author's poems conveys an impression of loneliness and sorrow. The personification (see Chapter 11) of love fleeing over the mountain and hiding 'amid a crowd of stars' (line 12) reinforces the sense of loss the woman must feel. The slow-moving iambic pentameter lines help establish the sense of the lethargy of old age. The imagery, metaphors and rhythm combine to create the sad and wistful tone the poem so appropriately conveys.

Resignation

The tone of some literary works will help convey the sense that, even if life is not ideal, it is necessary to accept the way things are. In other words, a writer will use tone to help convey a sense that he or she is resigned to the reality of a certain situation.

Example

William Shakespeare, 'When My Love Swears That She is Made of Truth'
The speaker of Shakespeare's Sonnet 138 expresses concern about his declining years and the consequent infidelity of his girlfriend. He knows she lies to him but he ostensibly believes her lies. She, in turn, flatters his youthful appearance when they both know he is well past his prime. They have an unspoken agreement: he will overlook her infidelity, and she will overlook the loss of his youth and vitality. In this way, they maintain their sexual relationship – 'lie' with each other – even while they tell lies to each other.

> Therefore I lie with her, and she with me,
> And in our faults by lies we flattered be.
>   (lines 13–14)

The relationship, obviously, is far from ideal, but it works because they both play the game.

The tone of this sonnet is one of resignation and acceptance. The speaker could be sad about his relationship with his friend, but he is not. The pun on the word 'lie' with which the sonnet concludes undercuts any sorrow he might have otherwise expressed. He is shrugging his shoulders and saying his relationship is far from perfect but better than having no relationship at all. The tone of the poem conveys this rather carefree and accepting, if not contented, attitude.

Irony

The tone of a work of literature is ironic when events do not unfold as they should, usually because a character refuses or is unable to recognise deception in another character or a deficiency in him or herself.

Example
Dorothy Parker, 'One Perfect Rose'
The speaker in the American writer Dorothy Parker's poem 'One Perfect Rose' describes the perfect rose 'with scented dew still wet' her admirer sends her. Along with the rose is a tender and endearing protestation of love. The irony is that a perfect rose is not what she wants, as the poem's final stanza makes clear:

Why is it no one ever sent me yet
One perfect limousine, do you suppose?
Ah no, it's always just my luck to get
One perfect rose.
    (lines 9–12)

The tone of this poem actually changes from beginning to end. It begins as a love poem with roses and heartfelt sentiment, and the diction – 'tenderly', 'deep-hearted', 'pure', 'love' – conveys a decidedly romantic tone. In the last stanza the tone changes with the phrase 'one perfect limousine' and becomes humorous and ironic. By the end of the poem, the one perfect rose has become a source of exasperation rather than a symbol of romance. Ironically, this woman prefers expensive presents over romantic ones.

Triumph

Literature is often inspirational. It tells of the power of faith, of courage overcoming seemingly insurmountable obstacles, of the strength of the human spirit. In such poems and stories, a triumphant tone is present.

Example
G. K. Chesterton, 'The Donkey'
Chesterton's poem is told from the point-of-view of the donkey who bemoans his homely physical appearance:

> The devil's walking parody
> On all four-footed things.
> (lines 7–8)

Other living things, the donkey continues, mock his discordant bray and foolish ears. But 'I also had my hour', the donkey continues: On Palm Sunday, it was upon my back that Christ rode into Jerusalem.

The tone of 'The Donkey' changes between the third and last stanza. In the first three stanzas the tone of the poem is rather bitter, as the donkey describes the torment he has endured. The diction – 'monstrous', 'sickening', 'tattered', 'scourge' – establishes this bitter tone. But, in the final stanza, the tone turns triumphant with the powerful image of the donkey bearing Christ into Jerusalem, while the people strew the way with palm branches and leaves. The tone helps to establish the theme of the poem: that physical beauty is irrelevant to the value of our actions.

Tutorial

Progress questions
1. In your own words, define the term 'tone' as an element of literature.

2. How can imagery be used to help a writer establish tone?

3. How can metaphor be used to help a writer establish tone?

4. How can diction be used to help a writer establish tone?

Seminar discussion
1. Complete this analogy: Tone is to a literary work as _____ is to _____.

2. Why do you think the tone of a literary work might change at some point?

Practical assignment
List ten adjectives (other than those discussed in this chapter) which could describe the tone of a literary work.

Study and revision tip
Consider the tone conveyed by the literary works on your reading list. Think about the ways in which the tone matches the writer's subject and theme.

15

The Reader's Point of View

One-minute overview – Your understanding of a literary work depends upon your knowledge of the genre in which the work is written, and the literary elements it contains. Interpretation also depends upon who you are. Indeed, contemporary literary theory stresses the role of the reader, as an equal partner to the writer, in creating the meaning of a text. **Reader response theory** asserts that the reader creates meaning and, because all people are different, all readings will be different. In its more extreme forms, literary theory asserts that there is no real meaning within a literary text. **Deconstruction** critics, for example, argue that, because language is an imperfect signifier of meaning, the meaning of a literary text always breaks down. Deconstruction critics look for those inconsistencies and ambiguities within a poem, story or play which undermine a unifying meaning. In other words, they 'deconstruct' – take apart – the text, believing that is the critics' main function. Many students of literature feel that deconstruction critics bite the hand that feeds them; the critics seem to take literary interpretation and analysis to extremes which show off their own ingenuity but do not help students comprehend. But by privileging the role of the reader, contemporary literary critics, as a group, do make literary analysis more relevant. Our gender, culture, age and political affiliation do affect our view of the world and, consequently, the way we read and understand literature. In this chapter we will explore the influences of:

- ▶ gender
- ▶ culture
- ▶ age
- ▶ politics.

The influence of gender

Our gender influences the way we read and understand literature. Women do not always interpret a literary work in the same way men do. If you are a feminist, you might interpret a literary work in a different way from other women.

Feminist literary criticism

Indeed, since the late 1960s, feminist literary criticism and analysis has emerged as an important contribution to literary theory. Feminist critics read literature primarily to examine the relationships between the male and female characters and the distribution of power within those relationships. Often the purpose of their analysis is to reveal the patriarchal nature of society, the ways in which men have organised the social order to perpetuate their own power and to ensure the subjugation of women. For example, the Duke who narrates Browning's 'My Last Duchess' (see Chapter 7) would represent, to feminist critics, the archetypal, the extreme, male chauvinist, who has his wife murdered because she is in insufficient awe of her husband's power.

Example

Bobbie Ann Mason, 'Shiloh'
'Shiloh' is a story about a young couple whose marriage is on the rocks. The husband, Leroy, was a trucker, but, because of an accident, he cannot drive any longer, and he remains at home. Tensions, hidden while Leroy spent so much time on the road, begin to surface as Leroy and his wife, Norma Jean, now spend so much time together. Norma Jean and Leroy were married when they were eighteen and Norma Jean was pregnant. The baby died of sudden infant death syndrome. They have been married for sixteen years, but they have never confronted together the pain of their baby's death and it remains an unspoken source of guilt. Leroy wants the relationship to work and dreams of building a log cabin for the two of them to settle down in. Norma Jean does not share Leroy's interest in building a log cabin. She has a job, she is getting herself physically fit, and she has started attending classes at the local community college. She is beginning to distance herself from her husband and from her domineering mother, Mabel, as well. On a

day trip to Shiloh, site of a famous civil war battle and now a tourist spot, Norma Jean tells Leroy the marriage is over.

Male and female responses to 'Shiloh'
Male and female readers tend to read 'Shiloh' somewhat differently, the differences being most obvious in responses to the character of Leroy.

1. Men tend to have some sympathy for Leroy. His log cabin might be more than a pipe dream if Norma Jean showed some interest and offered some support, instead of mocking him and insisting it can't be done. Leroy is trying; he appears more willing than Norma Jean to confront and talk about the main problem within the marriage: the unresolved emotional trauma caused by the baby's death.

2. Women readers tend to have less sympathy for Leroy. He won't look for work. He smokes too much marijuana. His log cabin is a game, a grown man's Lego set. He is thirty-four years old, but he is still acting like an eighteen-year-old. Norma Jean has to leave him so she can realise her own potential.

A feminist response to 'Shiloh'
Feminist readers would also condemn Leroy as a husband who is threatened by his wife's tentative steps toward emancipation, a man who tries to re-subjugate his wife by promising to build her a log cabin. The log cabin is a symbol of the material security men are supposed to provide for women, but, typically, a false symbol, existing only on paper and as a replica Leroy builds from popsicle (lollipop) sticks. Moreover, the town's authorities will not even permit the construction of a log cabin.

Feminist readers would also attack Norma Jean's mother, Mabel, as an accessory to the perpetuation of a male-dominated world. Mabel inspects Norma Jean's house and monitors her cooking to make sure her daughter fulfils her gender roles as a good wife and housekeeper. She refuses to let her thirty-four-year-old daughter smoke and punishes her when she catches Norma Jean doing so. Indeed, it is this episode which pushes Norma Jean over the edge and gives her the courage to leave her husband and stand up to her mother.

At Shiloh, Norma Jean tells Leroy things changed when Mabel caught her smoking. 'That set something off,' she says. Here Norma Jean's feminist consciousness, suppressed throughout the story, surfaces clearly and powerfully. Early feminists declared their emancipation by smoking openly. By refusing to allow her mother, a symbol of an outmoded approach to gender roles, to forbid her from smoking, Norma Jean establishes her own feminist credentials. She becomes truly emancipated. She wins the civil war, which Mason symbolises by setting the end of the story in Shiloh and by taking the town's name for the story's title. Norma Jean is free now to strike out on her own and fulfil her true role as a modern emancipated woman.

The influence of culture

Culture can also influence literary interpretation. Members of minority cultures, for example, usually have traditions and experiences foreign to members of the 'mainstream' culture, and these traditions and experiences can colour the way they read and understand a poem or story. If you are Asian or African, for example, you might see things an American might not.

Example
Amy Tan, 'A Pair of Tickets'
In 'A Pair of Tickets' by Amy Tan, a young Chinese-American girl travels to China to meet her half-sisters, twins whom her now dead mother had to abandon during the Japanese invasion in 1944. Born and raised in America, Jing-Mei had never considered herself Chinese. But as she leaves Hong Kong and arrives in Shenzhen, she is instantly aware of her Chinese identity. This sense of her Chinese identity intensifies as she meets her native Chinese family, especially her twin half-sisters with whom she instantly bonds, 'all hesitations and expectations forgotten'. Jing-Mei's mother was right: her Chinese identity 'is in your blood, waiting to let go'. Jing-Mei's father takes a Polaroid of the three girls together, and, as they watch it develop before their eyes, they see, in their combined images, the face of their mother.

'A Pair of Tickets' tells readers the extent to which ethnicity determines identity. Readers who are members of ethnic minorities, especially those who have visited homelands and who have met or been reunited with family, will read 'A Pair of Tickets' as insiders. They will identify with Jing-Mei and understand how much her experience in China means to her self-understanding and awareness. Other readers will have a different, but no less profound response. They will gain some insight into the difficulties their friends and neighbours, who are members of ethnic minorities, face adjusting and adapting to 'mainstream' society when their names and faces reveal their minority status. They learn, as well, how central a role ethnic identity plays in shaping the characters of these friends and neighbours. This response will evoke more envy than concern. In the course of the story Jing-Mei loses nothing of her American heritage and identity, but she gains a whole new heritage and identity. Everyone should be so lucky.

The influence of age

Perhaps you have had already the experience of re-reading something you read some years earlier and realising your interpretation and understanding of that work has changed. Perhaps you have re-read a poem you loved as a child but find superficial now; perhaps you have re-read a poem you could not understand before but now find profound. Maturity and life experiences change the way we view and understand the world and so, inevitably, alter the way we read. You and your grandfather or grandmother may well have some disagreements if you read and discuss the same literary work.

Example
Sylvia Plath, 'Mirror'
Sylvia Plath's poem, 'Mirror', describes a woman who is in despair because she looks at herself each morning in the mirror, which reflects back to her an inexorably ageing face. The mirror is personified (see Chapter 11) and acts as the poem's narrator. 'In me,' the mirror says, the woman 'has drowned a young girl, and in

me an old woman/Rises toward her day after day, like a terrible fish' (lines 17–18).

1. A young girl reading this poem might feel contempt rather than pity for the woman the mirror describes. In the prime of her youth and unconcerned about the possible loss of her beauty, this reader will probably have some trouble wondering what all the fuss is about.

2. On the other hand, an older woman, even if she feels the tears the woman sheds represent an overreaction, would be more sympathetic, having gone through the painful process herself. The older woman would identify with the woman the mirror 'drowns', while the young girl would not.

Now if the young girl reader happens to be a fashion model, she will understand better the woman's grief, because she knows that old age in the fashion industry is measured in different terms from those of society in general. By her late twenties, when her work begins to disappear, a model might feel she is beginning to get old. If, on the other hand, the reader is a feminist, she will have little sympathy for the woman because the woman is measuring her self-worth with the currency of beauty, which is the currency men have decided will be used to measure a woman's value.

'Mirror' is a good example of a reader-response poem, a poem whose meaning is mediated by the age, occupation and social values of its readers.

The influence of politics

A reader's political philosophy will also influence the way he or she reads and interprets a literary work. For example:

(a) If you always vote Labour, you might interpret a literary work in a different way from a friend who always votes Conservative.

(b) If you are on the left wing of the Labour Party, a Marxist, you might interpret a literary work in a different way from a moderate.

Marxist literary theory

Indeed, just as there is a feminist school of literary criticism which reads literature from a feminist perspective, so too there is a school of Marxist literary theory. Like feminist critics, Marxist critics examine the imbalance of power relationships among characters in literature. With feminist critics the imbalance of power is a matter of gender, but to Marxist critics it is a matter of social class.

Marxist critics read – or, to use the term now widely used in literary analysis, **interrogate** – a text to critique the social forces that produced or inspired it. A Marxist critic, for example, would read Lawrence's 'The Rocking Horse Winner' (see Chapter 8) as an indictment against a materialistic middle-class society so bent on acquiring goods that its members will sacrifice familial love, self-respect and even their health in pursuit of wealth.

Example

Allen Ginsberg, 'A Supermarket in California'
In this poem, Allen Ginsberg describes an experience he had shopping – or rather shoplifting – in a typical American supermarket. He finds himself inside this monument to American consumerism and feels like an alien among middle-class families doing their grocery shopping, loading their cars, and returning to their suburban houses.

(a) A conservative reader would probably be critical of the poem's narrator, condemn his shoplifting, his admiration for gay poet Walt Whitman, and the indolent attitude which has led to his rootless existence. By rejecting mainstream society, the narrator lies down in the bed of loneliness he has made for himself.

(b) A Marxist reader would probably view the narrator as something of a hero, a soldier in the war against corporate consumerism, who gets even with the capitalists by stealing from them. His alienation and loneliness is not sad or pathetic but symptomatic of a deliberate choice he has made, his protest against a social order he rejects. His rootless existence is a badge of honour, a mark of his refusal to join the middle class in the relentless quest for more, which can only mean that others will get less.

'A Supermarket in California' is a good example of a poem, the meaning of which changes diametrically, according to the political philosophy of its readers.

Tutorial

Progress questions

1. In your own words, describe reader response theory.

2. In your own words, define the term 'deconstruction' as it relates to literary interpretation and analysis.

3. In your own words, describe feminist literary theory.

4. In your own words, describe Marxist literary theory.

Seminar discussion
Who determines the true meaning of a literary text?

Practical assignment
Other current trends in literary interpretation and analysis, not covered in this chapter, include:

(a) psychoanalytic criticism
(b) new historicist criticism
(c) structuralist criticism.

Find out what the basic tenets of these schools of criticism and analysis are, and write some short notes.

Study and revision tip
Compile a list of those works on your reading list which would lend themselves to feminist interpretations, and those which would lend themselves to Marxist interpretations. Explain why these critical approaches would work effectively for these works.

Glossary of Literary Terms

Adage A traditional or proverbial saying.

Allegory A story in which the characters and events extend beyond the confines of their story to represent an object lesson to readers.

Alliteration The repetition of a consonant sound – 'storm strewn sea'.

Anapaest The anapaestic metre consists of a series of two unstressed sounds followed by a single stressed sound.

Antagonist Character whose dramatic role is to oppose the protagonist.

Archetype A general type of character which seems to have always existed and which everyone recognises – mother, father, son, daughter, lover, warrior, coward, saint, devil, and so on.

Archetypal plot A sequence of events forming a type of story which has recurred throughout the history of a civilisation, and with which most people are familiar; for example, a battle between good and evil.

Assonance The repetition of vowel sounds, as in 'rapid rattle' (Wilfred Owen).

Aural Describes how a poem appeals to our sense of sound, hearing.

Ballad A narrative poem, usually written in quatrains.

Blank verse Unrhymed iambic pentameter poetry.

Blocking agents In drama, characters who try to prevent things happening.

Camera work As a film term, refers to the direction (angle) in which the camera is pointed in relation to its subject, its movement (tilting, close up, zoom in, or panning, for example) the effects angle and movement produce.

Carpe diem Seize the day.

Catharsis The purging of audience emotion in tragedy, the release of emotion, and final feeling of relief.

Character One who lives within a poem, story or play.

Comedy Form of drama characterised by some sense of optimism, fellowship, love and good humour.

Conceit A metaphor which is unusually ingenious or elaborate.

Contextual symbol A symbol which has a non-literal meaning only within the context of the work of art in which it is found.

Continuity The extent to which a film's editor has transitioned effortlessly and without content errors from one scene to the next.

Couplet A two-line stanza.

Dactyl The dactylic metre is the opposite of the anapaestic. It consists of a series of a single hard-stressed sound followed by two soft-stressed sounds.

Deconstruction A school of literary criticism which seeks to take apart a text and its language to reveal other meanings. Some deconstructionists seem to take literary interpretation and analysis to extremes.

Depth of field Product of the cameras focus, referring to the visibility of characters and props in the foreground of a scene compared with the visibility of characters and props in the background of a scene.

Dramatic monologue A poem which is 'dramatic' in the sense that it is a speech presented to an audience (sometimes of only one person) and a 'monologue' in the sense that no other character does any talking.

Dynamic character Sometimes referred to as a round character, a dynamic character is one whose values, attitudes and/or ideals change as a result of the experience the character undergoes throughout the story.

Editing The work a film editor does to connect one scene to the next in the best interest of the film's narrative flow.

Egotist One who is convinced of his own importance and influence.

Elegy A poem written to commemorate the death of a person who played a significant role in the poet's life.

Epic A narrative poem, the length of a long novel. It has a traditional structure, typically opening in the middle of the action.

Epiphany A change, sudden insight or awareness revealed to the main character.

Eye rhyme Words which look as if they should rhyme but do not, for example 'good' and 'mood'. Also known as sight rhyme.

Fable A short and traditional story, often recounted, and involving archetypal characters in a moral setting.

Feminism and literature Feminist critics aim to examine the relationships between the male and female characters and the distribution of power within those relationships.

Fiction Prose text in the form of a story that is primarily a product of human imagination.

First-person major-character narrator This type of narrator is something of an egotist, telling a story in which he or she is the main character, or main focus of attention.

First-person minor-character This narrator is typically a gossip. He or she observes the actions of another person, often a friend, and then tells what that friend did, when, and to whom.

Flashback The technique of narrating an event which occurred before the point in the story to which the narrator has advanced.

Flat character A character, also known as a static character, who is offered the chance for positive change but who, for one reason or another, fails to embrace it.

Focus film term referring to comparative clarity of images in foreground and background.

Free verse Poetry without a set rhyme scheme or rhythm pattern.

Full rhyme The use of words which rhyme completely, such as 'good' and 'wood'.

Genre A widely accepted literary form, such as drama, poetry and the novel.

Haiku The Japanese haiku is a brief poem, consisting of a single image. The haiku consists of three lines of five, seven and five syllables, respectively.

Half rhyme Describes words which almost rhyme such as time and mine.

Hamartia In drama, the tragic hero has a character defect, called the tragic flaw or hamartia.

Horatian satire Named after the Roman poet, Horace, this is a fairly gentle type of satire used to poke fun at people and their failings or foibles.

Hyperbole A metaphor which bases its comparison on the use of exaggeration, for example, 'I'd walk a million miles for one of your smiles' (Al Jolson).

Iambic The iambic rhythm pattern in poetry consists of one unstressed sound or beat, followed by one stressed sound or beat.

Iambic dimeter A line with two beats.

Iambic pentameter A line with five beats.

Iambic tetrameter A line with four beats.

Iambic trimeter A line with three beats.

Imagery In literature, an image is a word picture. It can be a phrase, a sentence or a line. It is used to enhance the reader's appreciation of the figurative more than the literal meaning of a poem, story or play.

Imagists A group of poets whose aim between 1912 and 1917 was to write poetry which accented imagery or, their preferred term, 'imagism', to communicate meaning.

In media res Latin for 'in the middle of the action', the point at which an epic typically opens.

Irony The distance between what is supposed to happen and what actually happens.

Juvenalian satire Named after the Roman poet Juvenal, this form of satire uses bitter sarcasm more than humour, and is often tinged with cruelty.

Lighting As a film term, refers to the source of the light, the direction from which it comes, and the effects the source and direction produce.

Limited omniscient narrator A narrator who limits him or herself to relaying to readers the thoughts and actions of the main character only.

Litotes The deliberate use of understatement, usually to create an ironic or satiric effect.

Marxist literary theory Like feminist critics, Marxist critics examine the imbalance of power relationships among characters in literature, in terms of social class.

Metaphor A comparison intended to clarify or intensify the more complex of the objects of the comparison.

Metonymy A form of metaphor in which a phrase is understood to represent something more; for example, to use the phrase 'sabre rattling' to mean 'threatening war'.

Metre A term used to describe the rhythm and measure of a line of poetry.

Montage A series of very quick camera shots in rapid succession to create a particular cinematic effect, such as disorientation.

Narrative The storyline in a literary work.

Narrator Storyteller.

Non-sequential plot One in which the author holds back an important incident that occurred before the chronological ending of the story, typically to create suspense.

Novel A narrative work of fiction typically involving a range of characters and settings, linked together through plot and sub-plots.

Novella A short work of fiction which falls, in length, somewhere between the novel and the short story.

Objective narrator The objective narrator establishes setting in a precise but rather detached style, and then lets the conversation tell the story, using an objective point-of-view.

Octave An eight-line stanza.

Ode A long formal poem which tyically presents a poet's philosophical views about such subjects as nature, art, death and human emotion.

Omniscient narrator A narrator capable of telling readers the thoughts of all the characters and the actions of all the characters at any time. An omniscient narrator is like a god who can provide readers with all the information they could ever want.

Onomatopoeia A word or phrase usually found in a poem the sound of which suggests its meaning.

Oral Describes a spoken as opposed to written literary tradition.

Paradox A phrase which seems self-contradictory but, in fact, makes powerful sense despite its lack of logic.

Pastoral Relating to the countryside, especially in an idealised form.

Pastoral elegy A form of elegy that typically contrasts the serenity of the simple life of a shepherd with the cruel world which hastened the death of the poet's friend.

Personification A form of metaphor which compares something non-human with something that is human.

Petrarchan sonnet A sonnet with a rhyme scheme: abbaabbac-decde.

Plot In a literary fiction work, 'plot' refers to the events, the order in which they occur, and the relationship of the events to each other.

Poetry One of the major literary genres, usually written in a series of discrete lines which highlight the artistic use of language.

Point-of-view The stance from which the storyteller or narrator tells the story.

Prose The written text of fiction and non-fiction.

Protagonist The main character in a literary work. See also antagonist.

Quatrain A four-line stanza.

Reader response theory A theory of literature which asserts that the reader creates meaning and that, because all people are different, all readings will be different.

Regular verse A literary work written in lines which have the same rhythm pattern and a regular rhyme scheme.

Religious symbol A symbol used to suggest the need for faith or a crisis of faith that a main character is suffering.

Rhyme scheme The rhyming pattern of a regular-verse poem.

Rhyming couplet A two-line stanza in which the last words in each line rhyme.

Satire A literary form in which a writer pokes fun at those aspects of his society, especially those people and those social institutions which the author thinks are corrupt and in need of change.

Scapegoat A person who is banished or sacrificed in the interests of his community.

Sequential plot One in which the events are narrated in the order in which they occurred in time.

Sestet A six-line stanza.

Shakespearean sonnet A sonnet with a rhyme scheme: ababcdcde-fefgg.

Short story A prose fiction narrative, which usually occurs in a single setting, and concerns a single main character.

Sight rhyme Words which look as if they should rhyme but do not, for example 'good' and 'mood'. Also known as eye rhyme.

Simile A type of metaphor which makes the comparison explicit by using either the word 'like' or the word 'as'.

Sonnet A fourteen-line regular-verse poem, usually written in iambic pentameter.

Spondee A double-hard-stressed phrase such as 'shook foil' (Gerard

Manley Hopkins, 'God's Grandeur').

Static character A static character, also known as a flat character, is one who is offered the chance for positive change but who, for one reason or another, fails to embrace it.

Stereotype A recognisable *type* of person rather than a fully developed character. A stereotypical character is one who can be identified by a single dominant trait.

Symbolism The use within a literary work of an element which has more than a literal meaning.

Synecdoche The use of a part to represent a whole, as in the expression 'lend me a hand'.

Tercet A three-line stanza.

Theatre of the absurd A phrase used to describe a group of plays written during and after the 1950s. The term 'absurd' is used because the plots and the characters (though not the themes) are unconventional when examined in the context of conventional tragedy and comedy.

Theme The message or insight into human experience that an author offers to his or her readers. Broad themes might include family, love, war, nature, death, faith, time, or some aspect of these.

Tone The attitude or personality which a literary work projects; for example, serious and solemn, or light-hearted and amusing.

Tragedy A play which tells the story of a significant event or series of events in the life of a significant person.

Trochaic The opposite of iambic. The rhythm of the lines of a trochaic poem consist not of a series of soft-stress-hard-stress sounds, but a series of hard-stress-soft-stress sounds.

Valediction Bidding farewell to someone or something.

Verse A unit of a varying number of lines with which a poem is divided. Also called a stanza.

Villanelle A nineteen-line poem divided into five tercets and one quatrain.

Index of Authors and Titles

General Index